An Architectural Account Of The Churches Of Shropshire, Volumes 1-2

AN
ARCHITECTURAL
ACCOUNT
OF THE
CHURCHES
OF
SHROPSHIRE

HOBSON & CO. WELLINGTON, SHROPSHIRE.

AN ARCHITECTURAL ACCOUNT

OF

THE CHURCHES

OF SHROPSHIRE,

By the Rev.

D. H. S. CRANAGE, M.A., F.S.A.,

KING'S COLLEGE, CAMBRIDGE,

LECTURER ON ARCHITECTURE TO THE LOCAL EXAMINATIONS AND LECTURES
SYNDICATE OF THE UNIVERSITY OF CAMBRIDGE;

ILLUSTRATED WITH PERMANENT PLATES, REPRODUCED

FROM PHOTOGRAPHS BY

MARTIN J. HARDING,

MEDALLIST AT LONDON, VIENNA, CALCUTTA, &C.;

WITH GROUND PLANS OF THE MOST IMPORTANT CHURCHES,

DRAWN BY

W. ARTHUR WEBB, A.R.I.B.A.,

SILVER MEDALLIST OF THE ARCHITECTURAL ASSOCIATION, &C.

IN TWO VOLUMES.

(VOL. I.)

WELLINGTON, SHROPSHIRE.

HOBSON & Co.,

1901.

PUBLISHED BY SUBSCRIPTION.

FIVE HUNDRED COPIES PRINTED.

PART   I. PUBLISHED JULY, 1894.

PART   II. PUBLISHED JULY, 1895.

PART III. PUBLISHED FEBRUARY, 1897.

PART IV. PUBLISHED APRIL, 1900.

PART   V. PUBLISHED AUGUST, 1901.

MATRI   MEAE

CONSILIORUM   PARTICIPI

FAUTRICI   STUDIORUM

HOC   OPUS

PIETATIS   SIGNUM   GRATISSIMAE

D. D. D.

AUCTOR

FILIUS   AMANTISSIMUS.

PREFACE.

EIGHT years have gone by since I undertook to write "An Architectural Account of the Churches of Shropshire," and the first volume, published in five parts, is now completed. If I had realized the magnitude of the work, I fear that I should never have undertaken it. The gratifying reception that the first part met with, at the hands of antiquaries who were capable of judging, encouraged me to proceed, and I have gone on, earnestly endeavouring to make the history of each church as thorough and accurate as possible. The time and labour which the process has involved, I need not enlarge upon : only those who have undertaken similar work can fully sympathize with me. I cannot say that the book is absolutely free from mistakes, but my brother antiquaries have noticed very few. At the end of the work I propose to print an appendix, where they will be corrected, and where any additional information I have gleaned since the various churches were dealt with will be detailed. At the end, too, will be a lengthy article on the architecture of the county as a whole. The churches are first considered as units, but such treatment would be incomplete if there were not a final attempt to summarize. Generalizations are apt to be made on insufficient data ; but, if every church in a county has been visited, I think some architectural generalizations may be permitted.

I wish to emphasize the fact that the book is mainly an architectural one. It is a history of the fabrics of the churches, and not of the parishes or of the chief families which have inhabited them. But even with this limitation I have found it difficult to keep the book within reasonable bounds, as it seemed desirable that there should be some mention of ancient stained glass, tombs, bells and communion plate. I have made considerable reference to the first two of these, and in connection therewith have been tempted to refer at length to the heraldry. This, however, would have involved long genealogical discussions, which are foreign to my subject. Occasionally, as at Hopesay, a shield of arms throws light on the ancient history of the fabric, and it is then carefully explained. I have found it impossible to deal with the communion plate ; but, if a parish possesses anything specially remarkable, the fact is noted : there is very little pre-

Reformation plate in the county. Hardly anything is said about the bells, for a book is being written on the subject by Mr. H. B. Walters of the British Museum : this important work will soon be issued in instalments to the members of the Shropshire Archæological and Natural History Society. I have generally mentioned the year when a parish register commences. The valuable publications of the Shropshire Parish Register Society were not thought of eight years ago. Other subjects demand occasional notice, such as ancient tiles, sun-dials, fine yew trees ; but there is no pretence of dealing exhaustively with anything but the architecture.

Unfortunately there is rarely any MS. evidence of the early history of the fabric of a parish church. A careful study of the building itself and a comparison of it with dated examples are in nine cases out of ten the only means of ascertaining the history. Where, however, I have come across ancient documentary evidence, as at Tong, Ludlow, and Chelmarsh, I have of course given it very full consideration. Such evidence is usually detailed in the *Antiquities of Shropshire*, by the Rev. R. W. Eyton ; but Mr. Eyton often gives a lengthy history of a church without even mentioning the actual building. He had very little architectural knowledge, and never attempted to write the architectural history of a church. Indeed, with the exception of some notes of a few churches by the Rev. J. L. Petit, there is scarcely any mention of the fabrics at all. But, so far as Mr. Eyton goes, he is nearly perfect, and I gladly join with all other Shropshire antiquaries in expressing gratitude for his herculean labours and his splendid accuracy. Much light is sometimes thrown on the later history of an old church by churchwardens' accounts, and in some cases, as at Ludlow and Lydbury North, I have dealt with such evidence at great length.

The plan adopted in describing a church is to give first a general sketch of its history, and then to enter into details, and shew the evidence on which different parts of the building have been referred to different periods. The interior is first described, beginning with the chancel. The description of the exterior generally commences with the chief entrance and proceeds eastwards. An occasional departure from this arrangement of a church's history has been necessary.

In a literary work which is spread over many years, it is difficult to keep to the same style and plan throughout. Knowledge naturally increases and modes of expression alter. I hope it will be found that there is a fair degree of uniformity. I am conscious of one change in the later work,—the tendency to deal more fully with the history of a church during the 17th and 18th centuries. Years ago, one was perhaps too much taken up with enthusiasm for everything " Gothic," and was inclined to think that nothing later than the 16th century was of any account.

Further study has shown the absurdity of this, and has intensified one's hatred of much so called " restoration,"—a word which often means the sweeping away of everything that is not mediæval and the substitution of modern imitations of " Gothic " features. Anyone who has visited a large number of old churches is almost certain to become an anti-restorer, but I have tried to be fair to the other side. The pendulum may swing too far in the " anti-scrape " direction. It is easy enough to run down all restoration, but it has to be borne in mind that a church is not chiefly a museum of archæology, but a place of worship. It is no easy matter, when there are debased and inartistic additions, to say what must be retained for historical reasons, and what is unbearably ugly or irreverent. I am glad to testify that the problem has been solved by some architects and clergy with conservative care and common sense.

This is mainly an archæological work, but I have thought it well to make some mention of modern churches, especially as they some-times contain ancient features. Unconsecrated churches and iron buildings are not included.

I am aware that the attempt I have made to write for both the archæologist and the general reader cannot be perfectly successful. Sometimes the latter will be unable to follow a long and close argument, and often the former will think some information unnecessary. I have never shrunk from writing at great length if the point elaborated is of real importance in the history of a church, but I have tried to be interesting wherever it is possible. As a rule, I have not been content to state dogmatically that part of a church was built at a particular period, but have explained why this is so. The archæologist will not need the explanation, but the general reader may be glad of it. For the sake of the latter a glossary has been written. I hope this will not be criticized as a treatise on architecture, to which it has no pretensions. It is an explanation of the few technical terms in constant use, and a discussion of those architectural matters which are specially important in the county of Salop. Thus, the mouldings of capitals and bases are dealt with at some length, for such knowledge is extremely useful in parish churches; but the important subject of vaulting is dismissed in a few words, as there are hardly any vaulted roofs in the county. An exhaustive glossary is clearly impossible in a work of this kind. As a rule only those mediæval details which constantly occur are described, and no attempt is made to deal at length with the pre-Conquest and post-Reformation periods.

It will be noticed that the long-established nomenclature of Rickman is retained:—" Norman," " Early English," " Decorated," " Per-pendicular." I am aware of the grave objections to this and all other plans of dividing mediæval architecture. I know they are apt to encourage the notion that the styles are wholly different, instead of being steps in an orderly development; but I remain convinced that some division into styles is a necessity in a book of this kind, and that there is no sufficient reason to abandon the long-accepted system of Rickman. To give one illustration of my meaning. One sometimes comes across a Perpendicular feature which has nothing about it to indicate with certainty the early, middle, or late part of the period. Without the help of a division into styles, one must say, " It belongs to the latter part of the 14th century, or to the 15th century, or to the early part of the 16th century." With such help, one simply states, " It is Perpendicular."

It will be observed that the churches are dealt with under the different Hundreds, a division which seems to be suitable in an archæological work. I have had very unexpected difficulties in finding out in what Hundred certain churches were situated. I knew nothing about Hundreds when the work was commenced, and supposed that each place was unmistakably in some particular Hundred. I soon found that authorities differed very much on this point. The county is still divided into Hundreds for Petty Sessions and Coroners' business. For the former the arrangement departs widely from the usually accepted lines, and for the latter it is curiously uncertain with regard to some villages. One naturally looks therefore for a surer guide. I would gladly have taken Mr. Eyton's word as final, but he gives no help with regard to some modern churches; and, if a village is situated in two Hundreds, he does not say in which the parish church should be counted. I was forced therefore to consult old maps and directories, only to find that these constantly differed. Any one of them seemed to lead me wrong now and then. I could not therefore bind myself to any one guide, but decided what Hundred a church was in by the evidence which seemed best at the time. The arrangement must not be quoted as perfectly trustworthy, for I did not regard it as a part of my work to make an elaborate investigation into the precise limits of an almost obsolete partition. I adopted the division into Hundreds instead of Deaneries, because the book was archæological rather than ecclesiastical, and I am disappointed that it has landed me in such difficulties.

The volume now completed deals with the southern half of the county, but this is only a rough arrangement. Some of the Hundreds overlap one another considerably, and it is impossible to get an exact division. Two churches in the extreme south have not been described,— Dowles, and Middleton near Ludlow. Dowles is now in Worcestershire, and I therefore avoided it. Some time afterwards I found that Ludford had been put into Shropshire, and I had regarded it as in Herefordshire. As the change was made after the first part of this book was published, I think I had better include Dowles and not Ludford. The church will be described in the appendix, and also Middleton, which was omitted owing to a misunderstanding as to its Hundred.

The spelling of the place-names is another thing which varies considerably. I have followed that of the Ordnance Map of 1833, the latest complete Ordnance Map at the time my book was commenced. To this rule there are I think only four exceptions. "Bridgnorth," "Coalbrookdale," "Ironbridge," "Oakengates" had become so established that I did not suspect that the map of 1833 printed them "Bridgenorth," "Coalbrook Dale," "Iron Bridge," "Oaken Gates." The churches of each hundred are arranged alphabetically. Place-names which are qualified by "Great," "Little," or equivalent words, will not be found under "G," "L" etc., but under the initial letters of their more specific names. Thus, "Much Wenlock," "Little Wenlock" are put under "W." On the other hand, it has seemed better to put "Church Stretton" under "C," "Hope Bowdler" under "H": a similar course has been adopted with other double names such as Acton Scott.

To my coadjutors, Mr. Martin J. Harding and Mr. W. A. Webb, I owe more than I can express. They have thought no amount of trouble and time too much to produce the best results, and they have done their work without reward. No man was ever more fortunate in his colleagues than I have been.

It is only fair to Mr. Harding to say that I am responsible for the choice of subjects to be illustrated, and for the point of view from which the photographs were taken. A more artistic picture could often have been made if archæological considerations had been sacrificed. The plan adopted throughout is to illustrate freely where there are features of special interest, and, where this is not so, to give no illustrations at all. The financial difficulty would alone prevent one giving a picture of every church. It is necessary to point out that some of the photographs are not distorted because they appear to be so. The walls of an old church are not always upright, and lines which a modern builder would make parallel are often very much the reverse in old work : such irregularities are carefully recorded in the photographs. All the illustrations are printed in permanent ink. The large plates are collotypes, the plans and small figures in the text are reproduced by the Meisenbach process.

Mr. Webb has drawn all the plans and nearly all the sections of mouldings, etc., in the text. For the choice of these and the marks of date attached to them I am entirely responsible. The system of hatching throughout the book is uniform, with the exception of the plan

on page 114, where the black lines do not indicate Norman work. A
reference is appended.

REFERENCE .

▥ Saxon.	▦	Decorated.
■ Norman.	▨	Perpendicular Early.
▢ Norman Late.	▧	Perpendicular.
▤ Early English Early.	▧	Perpendicular Late.
▥ Early English.	⬚	1538~1700.
▦ Early English Late.	▱	18ᵗʰCentury.
▨ Decorated Early.	☐	Modern.
▨ Decorated.		

There is no place in the system for a Transition period. " Norman Late " is
directly succeeded by " Early English Early." It is sometimes difficult
to know which mark to use, for there was no definite break between
the two periods. If in Decorated work, for example, there are traces of
Early English feeling still remaining, the mark " Decorated Early " is
used : if there are signs of the Perpendicular style coming on,
" Decorated Late " is the hatching : if the work belongs to the middle of
the period, or else, though clearly of the style named, has no proof of
early or late date, " Decorated " only is employed. When once the system
is mastered, it will, I think, be found a great convenience, in reference
to the sections and the plans. Such plans are of the greatest help in
understanding the history of a building : they are supplied of all the
more important churches. Some of the plans are reduced more than
others. For example, the plan of a large church like Ludlow occupies as
much room as the size of the page will allow. If Chelmarsh had been

dealt with in the same way, a very small part of the page would have been used : this would have been a drawback, and the plan is therefore less reduced. In each case, the scale will be found at the side, and a comparison of the size of the churches can be made. The right hand side is always the east. In some cases, a good deal of Mr. Webb's time has been saved by the loan of plans which had already been carefully measured by architects. It seemed unnecessary to do all the measuring over again, but in each case the main points were verified by Mr. Webb or myself. In this connection I express my grateful thanks to the following :—the Rev. J. H. Courtney Clarke for a plan of Tong, Mr. C. Hodgson Fowler for his plan of Bromfield, the late Sir Arthur Blomfield for his plan of Alveley, Mrs. Baldwyn-Childe for a plan of Kinlet, the late Rev. W. Heaton for a plan of Morville, Mr. T. Blashill for his plan of Stottesdon, Mr. J. T. Micklethwaite for his plan of Lydbury North, and Mr. A. E. Street for his late father's plan of Clun.

The problems of mediæval architectural history which the churches suggest I have generally had to work out unaided, but great help has been received from the clergy in reference to the recent changes and restorations, the dates of the parish registers, and other details. From almost every beneficed clergyman in south Shropshire I have had some assistance of this kind, and to many I owe a great debt of gratitude for hospitality, and for much trouble willingly undertaken on my behalf. To my friend the Rev. W. G. Clark-Maxwell I must specially express my warm thanks, not only for the kind of help just mentioned, but for some valuable archæological suggestions, especially in reference to Bromfield, Clunbury, Hopesay, and Lydbury North churches. He also very kindly looked through part of the Lydbury North churchwardens' accounts, and reduced the time, very great even then, which I had to spend on those documents. From several of the laity, who took special interest in particular churches, I have also received considerable assistance, chiefly by their recollections of what the buildings were like before " restoration." Among these should be mentioned :—Mr. Edmund Jones for help in reference to Ludlow, the late Colonel Capel Cure for Badger, Mr. T. H. Thursfield for Barrow, Colonel Wakeman for Alveley, Viscountess Boyne for Burwarton, Mrs. Wooler for Cleobury North, Mr. Warenne Fitz Warren for Morville, Mrs. Rocke for Clungunford. To Mrs. Baldwyn-Childe of Kyre Park I owe a special debt. She most kindly placed at my disposal all her papers and sketches dealing with the condition of Cleobury Mortimer and Kinlet churches during the last 40 years. She also supplied me with a good deal of unpublished information with regard to the Kinlet family. I am indebted to the late Mr. J. Townshend Brooke of

Haughton Hall for repeated permission to examine the sketches of his father, the Rev. J. Brooke, who drew most of Eyton's illustrations. These are contained in twenty-two large volumes, mostly concerned with Shropshire subjects, especially churches. They are of priceless value, as shewing the condition of the churches before modern "restoration" took place. I must also express my thanks to Mr. H. C. Beddoe, Deputy Registrar of the Diocese of Hereford, for the opportunity of looking through his valuable collection of drawings of churches in south Shropshire. I have been helped with regard to one or two heraldic and other matters by Mr. W. H. St. John Hope, who is always so unselfishly ready to place his great knowledge at the disposal of other antiquaries. My friends the Rev. A. R. F. Hyslop and Mr. E. H. Blakeney have been good enough to help me in some matters of scholarship and literary expression. The latter has also made some valuable suggestions with regard to typographical details,—a kind of help I have also received from Mr. R. D. Radcliffe. My indebtedness to Mr. Mill Stephenson's admirable "Monumental Brasses in Shropshire" has already been expressed. There are some suggestive descriptions of the misericords at Ludlow in Mr. Oliver Baker's "Ludlow Town and Neighbourhood." A very useful article should be mentioned on "Some Shropshire Briefs" by the Hon. and Rev. G. H. F. Vane in the Transactions of the Shropshire Archæological and Natural History Society, 2nd series, vol. XI. To the Council of that Society, and especially to the Chairman, the Rev. T. Auden, I wish to express my sense of their continued support and encouragement. Other assistance is recognized here and there in the text. If I have omitted to mention anyone to whom acknowledgments are due, I hope it will be put down to an oversight and not to ingratitude.

Last, but far from least, I must express my heartfelt gratitude to my publisher, Mr. Hugh Hobson, for his unwearied patience in dealing with the scores of difficulties entailed by the publication of such a book. His invariable courtesy and encouragement have often lightened the load which every author must feel, whose work extends over several years.

For the present I take leave of the large number who have been good enough to subscribe to my book. Interruptions from ill health and the pressure of parochial and other duties have delayed the publication of this first volume. I have good hopes that the second will be completed in a much shorter space of time.

MUCH WENLOCK.   D. H. S. CRANAGE.
July, 1901.

CONTENTS.

The Franchise of Wenlock.

The Hundred of Overs.

The Hundred of Stottesdon.

The Hundred of Purslow.

The Hundred of Clun.

PLATES.

GROUND PLANS.

OTHER ILLUSTRATIONS.

GLOSSARY.

ABACUS. The uppermost division of a capital. It frequently reveals some clear sign of date. The simplest form of Norman abacus is shewn in

Fig. A.   *Fig. B*   *Fig. C.*

Fig. A. This, however, may occur at any period. The small quirk or channel shewn in Fig. B marks the abacus a distinctly Norman work. This may be combined with a hollow chamfer, as in Fig. C. Figs. B and C are exceedingly common in the county of Salop. The quirk sometimes

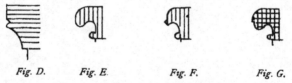

Fig. D.   *Fig. E.*   *Fig. F.*   *Fig. G.*

survives into the early part of the Early English period, but the lower part of it becomes curved, as in Fig. D. Early English abaci are generally curved at the top and undercut, as in Figs. E and F. The undercutting distinguishes them from the capitals of all other periods. A small fillet is often added to the upper part, as in Fig. F. Towards the end of the period the scroll moulding comes in and is often combined with the undercutting, as in Fig. G. In the Decorated period the scroll

Fig. H.   *Fig. I.*

moulding is far the most frequent (Fig. H). Perpendicular abaci generally begin with a slope and have an ogee below (Fig. I). About the middle of the 14th century the Decorated form gradually changes into the Perpendicular, and it is often quite impossible to tell whether an abacus is late Decorated or early Perpendicular.

The shape of the abacus varies. In the Norman period it is always square on small capitals and generally so on large ones. In the Early English style it is most frequently circular, but sometimes octagonal. The Decorated abacus is circular or octagonal as a rule, and the Perpendicular abacus is nearly always octagonal.

ARCADE.　　A series of arches blind or open.

ARCH.　　A number of blocks so arranged as to support one another by mutual pressure, and to bear a weight placed on them. The term is also employed to describe one piece of material if it is shaped in the form of an arch. In the former and stricter sense, an arch has an outward pressure, and requires some kind of abutment on either side to support it. Most Norman arches are round, but all round arches are not Norman. They are common in the early part of the 13th century, very rare in the 14th century, and occur occasionally in the 15th century. In the late Perpendicular period they are fairly common. The origin of the pointed arch is a vexed question and cannot be discussed here. The chief reasons for its introduction in buildings of the 12th century were undoubtedly its convenience in vaulting and its weight-bearing power. Late Norman arches are often pointed, and pointed arches are the rule in the 13th, 14th, and 15th centuries. They are of many kinds, the most common being equilateral, drop, and lancet arches. The equilateral arch

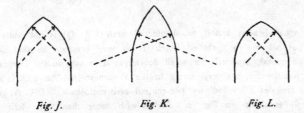

Fig. J.　　　　　　　*Fig. K.*　　　　　　　*Fig. L.*

(Fig. J) is described from two centres taken on the points of springing : its base is equal to one of its sides (the term " side " signifying the side of the triangle inscribed in the arch). The lancet arch (Fig. K) is described from two centres taken outside the points of springing : its base is less than one of its sides. The drop arch (Fig. L) is described from two centres taken inside the points of

springing : its base is greater than one of its sides. The segmental arch
(Fig. M) is used all through the Middle Ages, and the segmental pointed arch
(Fig. N) from about 1200 onwards, especially in the 13th and 14th centuries.

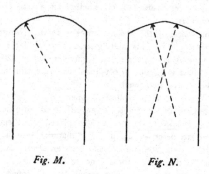

Fig. M.   *Fig. N.*

The trefoil arch was introduced in the Transitional period. It is of many
forms, round or pointed. Two varieties are shewn in Figs. O and P.

Fig. O.   *Fig. P.*   *Fig. Q.*

The square-headed trefoil or shouldered arch (Fig. Q) is not really an
arch at all but a corbelled lintel. It is very common in the Early
English period, especially for small doorways: it is used in the Decorated
style occasionally, but very rarely in the Perpendicular. An arch is said
to be trefoil*ed* if an ordinary two-centred arch encloses a trefoil. A good
example is shewn in Fig. 2. Arches with more than three foils are
frequent: the commonest is the cinquefoil. An arch is stilted if the
lower part of it on each side is a straight vertical line. An ogee arch,
composed of contrasted curves (Fig. R), was common in the 14th and
15th centuries for small canopies over niches and sedilia. Three-centred
and four-centred arches (Figs. S and T) mark the Perpendicular style.

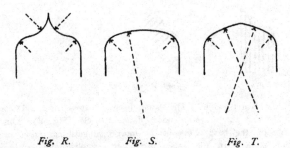

Fig. R.   *Fig. S.*   *Fig. T.*

The latter is exceedingly common, particularly for doorways.

ASHLAR.   Squared stone, as opposed to unsquared stone, which is called rubble.

AUMBRY.   A cupboard.   The term is usually applied to the cupboard for containing the sacramental vessels, which is generally in the north wall of a church.

BALL-FLOWER.   See ORNAMENT.

BARGE-BOARD.   A board, plain or ornamental, used up the sides of an overhanging gable, especially on porches.

BASE.   The lower part of a pier or column is often more characteristic than the capital.   Norman bases are very simple as regards their

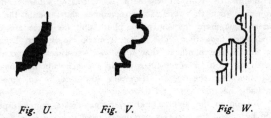

Fig. U.   *Fig. V.*   *Fig. W.*

mouldings (Fig. U is a common form), but they are often ornamented with carving.   In the late Norman period the Attic base becomes common (Fig. V) and naturally leads to the base shewn in Fig. W, which has the water-hollow so characteristic of the Early English style.   Another common Early English base has two or three rounds, as in Fig. X,

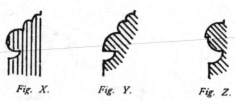

Fig. X.   Fig. Y.   Fig. Z.

without the water-hollow. The same form is used in the Decorated period, only that the lowest round is flat underneath (Fig. Y). This flat under-edge of the base is one of the most distinguishing marks of the Decorated style. In the same period the scroll moulding is used frequently for the base as well as the abacus (Fig. Z). In the latter

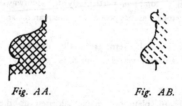

Fig. AA.   Fig. AB.

part of the Decorated period the undeveloped bell-shaped base is very common (Fig. AA) and leads to the bell-shape, which is almost universal in the Perpendicular period (Fig. AB).

The part below the base, which is generally unmoulded, is called the plinth. In Norman times it was usually square and of a greater projection than the base. It is sometimes the same in the Early English period, but more frequently the plinth and the base are of the same shape and projection. The latter remark applies to Decorated bases also, though the plinth at that time was sometimes octagonal and narrower than the base. Perpendicular plinths are generally octagonal and of less projection than the bases. Beginning low and broad, mediæval plinths gradually became high and narrow.

BAY. A division in the architectural arrangement of a church, especially that marked by one of the arches separating a nave from an aisle.

BEAD. A small round moulding.

BOSS. A projecting ornament of wood or stone, frequently placed at the intersections of roof ribs.

BOWTELL. See MOULDING.

BROACH SPIRE. A spire which rises straight from a tower without a parapet.

BUTTRESS. A projecting mass of masonry for extra strength and especially for resisting the outward pressure of an arch. If a buttress has an outward thrust to meet, projection is more important than breadth, and late buttresses are therefore more scientific than early ones. The Norman buttress is broad and of slight projection. Early English buttresses are narrower but still generally of greater breadth than projection in their upper parts. In the Decorated period buttresses are roughly square at the top. Perpendicular buttresses usually have greater projection than breadth. These are useful general rules but there are many exceptions. Norman buttresses have rarely more than one stage : later examples may have two or more. At the corners of churches two buttresses are often placed at right angles. At the end of the Early English period diagonal buttresses at corners were introduced, but the old arrangement was often continued all through the later styles.

CAMBER. See ROOF.

CANT. See ROOF.

CAPITAL. The top part of a column. It is divided into three parts, the abacus, the bell, and the neck. The first-named has been already dealt with. The bell is the usual part of a capital for ornamental carving. In the Norman period the variety of such carving is endless. The simplest form is the cushion capital, which is generally early, but sometimes survives comparatively late in the period. The most characteristic Norman capital is the scolloped (Plate L.). It does not occur in the earliest Norman work, but is very common for the first 80 years of the 12th century. Towards the end of the Norman period the capital is often cut into the shape of rude leaves, which sometimes end in volutes (Plate XXXVI.). The characteristic Early English capital is carved with "stiff-leaf foliage" (Plate XXXVIII.). Stiff-stalk foliage would be a more correct term. The leaves are far from stiff very often, and yet seem very appropriate to stone work. It has been beautifully said that if leaves ever had grown in stone they would have been like these leaves. In the Decorated style the leaves are closely copied from nature. In the Perpendicular period they are more formal and square and look as if they were stuck on the capital, instead of growing out of it as in the earlier styles.

In the three pointed periods the bell is frequently not carved but moulded. The varieties are endless, but the indications of date are not so distinct as on the abacus (see Figs. 1, 4, 5, 6, 8, 28, 32, 37, 39).

The lowest member of the capital, called the neck, generally has one moulding only, and the bead is the commonest form. In the Norman period the semi-hexagon is often seen and less frequently in the next style. The Decorated neck is very commonly the scroll.

Speaking generally, the Early English capitals have the greatest projection and the Perpendicular the least.

CHAMFER. See MOULDING.

CHANTRY. An endowment for saying masses. In the Middle Ages, especially in the century preceding the Reformation, it was a common custom for a man to leave money to ensure masses being said for the souls of himself and his friends. Part of the church, generally in a transept or aisle, was set apart for this purpose, or else a special addition was made to the building. The chapel thus formed is called a chantry chapel.

CINQUEFOIL. See WINDOW.

CLERESTORY. In a parish church this term applies to a row of windows over the arcade separating the nave from an aisle.

COLLAR. See ROOF.

CORBEL. A projecting support, generally of stone. A number of these joined together is called a corbel-table.

CREDENCE. See PISCINA.

CROCKET. A projecting leaf used especially up the sides of canopies and pinnacles. It is rare in the Early English period. Decorated and Perpendicular crockets are exceedingly common. The former partake of the natural leaf character. The latter are generally of a square outline (see Fig. 17 and Plate XXIX.).

CURVILINEAR. See WINDOW.

CUSP. See WINDOW.

DECORATED. See GOTHIC.

DENTILS. Ornaments resembling teeth, frequently used in Renaissance and later building, and derived from Grecian architecture.

DOG-TOOTH. See ORNAMENT.

DRIPSTONE. See HOOD-MOULDING.

EARLY ENGLISH. See GOTHIC.

EASTER SEPULCHRE. An imitation tomb frequently placed in a recess in the north wall of a chancel. On Good Friday evening an image of our Lord, with the consecrated host, was solemnly interred there and removed with great pomp on Easter morning.

FILLET. See MOULDING.

FINIAL. The ornament at the top of a canopy, pinnacle, etc.

FLAMBOYANT. See WINDOW.

FLUTINGS. Hollows cut vertically on columns.

FOIL. See WINDOW.

GARGOYLE. A projecting water-spout.

GOTHIC. This term was probably first applied to mediæval architecture in derision by the Classical school of the 17th century. The name

is now so thoroughly established that one is almost obliged to use it,
though it is really unsuitable. Gothic architecture has nothing to do with
the Goths. Different writers use the word in different senses. Some
include under it all English architecture from the Conquest to the
Reformation. Some refer it to pointed architecture only : others use it in a
still narrower sense. I have generally employed it in its most common
meaning,—to refer to pointed architecture from the end of the 12th to the
early part of the 16th century. For the purpose of this short article I will
take it in the broader sense first mentioned.

    The usually accepted division of mediæval architecture is that
of Rickman, one of the chief pioneers of the Gothic Revival in the early
part of the 19th century. It has its faults, like any other system of
nomenclature, but I cannot see that there is sufficient reason to discard it,
and I have therefore fallen in with the long-established custom. It is as
follows. I have slightly altered the dates, which are of course only
approximate.

1060 — 1180	Norman.
1180 — 1270	Early English.
1270 — 1370	Decorated.
1370 — 1520	Perpendicular.

One style always overlaps its successor by a few years, the period being
called a "Transition." If the word "Transition" is used without any
qualification, the period between Norman and Early English is referred to :
the whole of the latter half of the 12th century is sometimes included under
the term. The other Transitional periods are not quite so long, though,
for example, there is Perpendicular work before the middle of the 14th
century.

    Sometimes the last three of the above periods are called First
Pointed, Second Pointed, Third Pointed, or Early Pointed, Middle Pointed,
and Late Pointed respectively. Sharpe proposed the following division.
It is better than Rickman's in some respects, but has not superseded it.

449 — 1066	Saxon	} Romanesque.
1066 — 1145	Norman	
1145 — 1190	Transitional	
1190 — 1245	Lancet	
1245 — 1315	Geometrical	} Gothic.
1315 — 1360	Curvilinear	
1360 — 1550	Rectilinear	

There is no generally accepted nomenclature of post-Reformation
architecture. The most usual terms suggest their own meaning :—
Elizabethan, Jacobean, Queen Anne, Georgian. The term "Renaissance"

is applied to the revival of Classical forms in the early part of the 17th century. Gothic architecture languished but never wholly died out. In the last generation it was studied with extraordinary zest, and the Gothic Revival was the result.

HAGIOSCOPE.   See SQUINT.

HAMMER-BEAM.   See ROOF.

HERRING-BONE WORK.   Masonry laid in a slanting manner, alternate rows being placed the opposite way to each other.

HOOD-MOULDING.   A projecting moulding over the heads of arches, windows, and doorways. When used externally it is also called a dripstone, as it protects what is below it from the rain. For the mouldings of this feature see STRING-COURSE.

IMPOST.   The masonry from which an arch springs, whether in the form of a capital or otherwise.

JAMB.   The side of a window, doorway, etc.

KING-POST.   See ROOF.

LANCET.   See ARCH and WINDOW.

LYCH-GATE.   A covered entrance to a churchyard, used as a resting-place for the coffin at funerals.

LONG-AND-SHORT WORK.   Stones which are long vertically, placed alternately with others either long or short horizontally, especially at the corners of walls. It is a mark of pre-Norman building.

LOW SIDE WINDOW.   A window low down in the wall, which has originally had a shutter, especially for its lower portion. The position is nearly always the western part of the south wall of a chancel, but it is sometimes found in the north or east wall. These windows have given rise to endless discussion. The idea that they had anything to do with lepers or the practice of confession has been given up by almost every antiquary. One theory is that lamps were placed inside them to scare away evil spirits from the churchyard. Another suggestion is that they were used for ringing the sanctus bell therefrom at the time of mass.

MASK.   A corbel so carved that its shadow resembles the human face. It is very common in the 13th century, and not rare in the 14th.

MISERERE or MISERICORD.   A projecting bracket, often carved in a grotesque manner, under the seats of chancel stalls.

MOULDING.   A knowledge of mouldings is all-important in deciding the date of mediæval buildings. The following remarks refer chiefly to arches and the jambs of windows and doorways. Other mouldings are described under the headings ABACUS, BASE, CAPITAL.

Norman mouldings are very simple (ornamental mouldings are of course not referred to) and consist chiefly of rounds and hollows. In the

Early English style the hollows are deep and frequent: all the mouldings are drawn with the free hand. Decorated mouldings are more geometrical, especially in the early part of the period: the hollows are less numerous. In a Perpendicular set of mouldings there is generally one broad and shallow hollow: the mouldings themselves are shallow and run into one another with no distinct break between the members. Early English and early Decorated mouldings are almost always worked on receding squares as in Fig. 14, L: this arrangement survives from Norman doorways, with their receding orders. Late Decorated and Perpendicular mouldings are placed on one plane, sloping from the face of the arch to its centre.

The varieties of mediæval mouldings are endless. A few of the chief forms only are mentioned.

1. The plain roll, round or bowtell. This may be half a circle as in Fig. AC, or three-quarters of a circle or of other forms. It occurs at all periods.

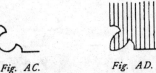

Fig. AC.   Fig. AD.

2. The pointed bowtell or pear (Fig. AD). This is most common in the Early English period, especially in the earlier part of it. When used in the Decorated style its base is generally broader than in the Early English.

3. The fillet. A small moulding, generally square-edged, used to separate others, and also worked on the top of others. It was introduced in the Transition period. The roll and fillet is a frequent combination. At first the two are quite distinct, though combined (Fig. AE).

Fig. AE.   Fig. AF.   Fig. AG.

In the latter half of the 13th and in the 14th century the two began to run into one another (Fig. AF), and in the 15th they are often inseparable (Fig. AG). This is only a general tendency: there are plenty of exceptions to the rule.

4. The scroll. In some parts of the country this was introduced late in the 12th century. In Shropshire it is not seen till about the middle of

the 13th century and then it is rare. It is the characteristic moulding of the Decorated style. When used in the Early English period the outline is

Fig. AH.   *Fig. AI.*   *Fig. AJ.*   *Fig. AK.*

roughly oval and there is a very slight break between the two parts (Figs. AH and AI). The Decorated scroll is more geometrical and has a distinct break between the parts (Fig. AJ).

5. The sunk quarter-round is similar to the scroll and also characteristic of the Decorated style (Fig. AK).

6. The chamfer is used at all periods. It is a corner cut off, i.e., Fig. AL becomes Fig. AM.

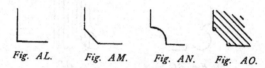

Fig. AL.   *Fig. AM.*   *Fig. AN.*   *Fig. AO.*

The hollow chamfer (Fig. AN) is also used all through the Middle Ages. The sunk chamfer (Fig. AO) is characteristic of the Decorated style.

7. The wave moulding is sometimes called the swelled chamfer. In the Decorated period the convex part is broad and slightly bulging (Fig. AP).

Fig. AP.   *Fig. AQ.*

In the Perpendicular, it is narrower and projects further (Fig. AQ). The concave parts are more decided in the latter than in the former.

8. The ogee. A moulding composed of two contrasted curves. Two mouldings together in the Early English style often look like an ogee, but the ogee proper is characteristic of the Decorated and Perpendicular. The double ogee is the combination of two ogees, forming a bracket. In the Decorated style the convex part is greater than the concave (Fig. AR). In the Perpendicular the two parts are about equal (Fig. AS). In the former case the ogee reminds one of half a roll and fillet, from which it

may have been derived. The combination of ogee and hollow chamfer (Fig. AT) is characteristic of the Perpendicular period.

Fig. AR. *Fig. AS.* *Fig. AT.*

If the reader will take the trouble to master the above rules he will find that he is able thereby to date a large number of mediæval buildings.

MULLION. The wood or stone division between the openings of windows, screens, etc. In parish church windows these are generally very plain. In the Decorated period they are simply chamfered. In the Perpendicular, they usually have hollow chamfers.

MULTIFOIL. See WINDOW.

NECK. See CAPITAL.

NEWEL STAIRCASE. A circular staircase winding round a central column.

NORMAN. See GOTHIC.

OGEE. See MOULDING.

ORNAMENT. Ornamental carving is most profuse in the Norman period. Later on, architectural effect was often obtained by rich moulding with very little ornament. It is impossible here to attempt a description of the endless varieties of mediæval ornament. The most characteristic of the various periods

Fig AU. *Fig. AV.* *Fig. AW.*

are :—zig-zag or chevron of the Norman, dog-tooth of the Early English (Fig. AU), ball-flower of the Decorated (Fig. AV), Tudor flower of the Perpendicular (Fig. AW).

PERPENDICULAR. See GOTHIC.

PISCINA. A ceremonial water-drain, nearly always placed on the south side of an altar and in an arched recess. The basins of early piscinas are generally deeper than those of the Perpendicular period. The arches are often moulded and ornamented in an elaborate manner. Frequently, however, in plain churches there is no detail about a piscina which fixes its date. Above the basin there often is, or has been, a shelf of stone or wood: this acted as a credence table, to receive the sacramental vessels and the elements before consecration. As every altar seems to have had its own piscina in the Middle Ages, there are often several remaining in a large church.

PLINTH. The lowest part of a column : its form is described under BASE. The term is also applied to the basement or base-moulding of a wall, which often has some detail to fix its date. One of the commonest forms in south Shropshire is shewn in Fig. 14, A. This nearly always marks the Transition from Norman to Early English.

PURLIN. See ROOF.

PUTLOG HOLES. Small holes in which scaffold poles have been placed : sometimes these have never been filled up.

QUATREFOIL. See WINDOW.

QUEEN-POST. See ROOF.

QUIRK. See ABACUS.

QUOIN. The external corner of a building. The term is also applied to the corner stones.

RAFTER. See ROOF.

REBATE. A small square-edged recess in which a casement or shutter fits.

REREDOS. The ornamental screen or stone-work behind an altar.

RESPOND. A half-pillar, used especially in single arches and at the ends of the arcade separating the nave from an aisle.

RETICULATED. See WINDOW.

ROOD. A cross or crucifix. This was often placed on a beam at the entrance of a chancel, accompanied by images of the Virgin Mary and St. John. Late in the 12th century, high screens were introduced in this position, surmounted by a small gallery which contained the rood. Thus we speak of a ROOD SCREEN and ROOD LOFT. They are very rare in parish churches before the 14th century, and the large majority date from the Perpendicular period. The lofts were often approached by a stone staircase, which frequently remains. The lofts themselves were nearly all taken down at the Reformation, but the screens were ordered to be preserved : many have been removed since that time.

ROOF. There are many different kinds of wooden roofs in churches. The most common types only are mentioned here. Roofs are single-framed or double-framed. The former are called trussed-rafter roofs, because every set of rafters is trussed or joined together. Fig. AX is an example with seven sides or cants.

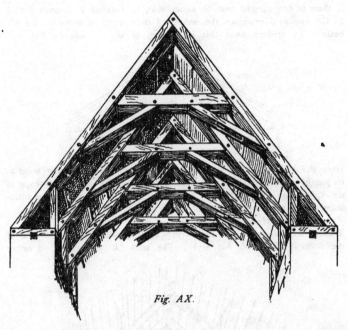

Fig. AX.

A waggon-headed appearance is given when the roof is boarded (Plate XXVII.). This is still more the case when the rafters are curved. Trussed-rafter roofs were introduced towards the end of the 12th century, and were common in the 13th and 14th centuries.

Double-framed roofs have a set of rafters joined together at certain points and called a truss: the intermediate beams rest on the trusses. Three main divisions may be made.

1. Tie-beam roofs.

In these, which were used all through the Middle Ages, the tendency of the sloping sides to spread outwards is counteracted by tie-beams stretched across the building at the points where the roofs spring (Plate XXXIV.). Frequently the tie-beam is slightly higher in the centre than at the sides: it is then said to be cambered (Plate X.). When the roof is nearly flat and the tie-beam is cambered, there is scarcely any space between the tie-beam and the ridge of the roof (Plate XXVI.). If one upright post is placed on the tie-beam in the centre, the roof is called a king-post roof (Plate XVIII.).

If there is one upright post on either side, it is called a queen-post roof. In the mediæval examples, the weight of these posts is borne by the tie-beam. In modern roofs this is not so, as will be seen by Fig. AY.

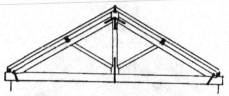

Fig. AY.

Here the king-post helps to lift up the tie-beam and to transfer some of its weight to the principal rafters and so to the walls: the wedge-shape of the upper part of the king-post should be noted. This device was introduced in the 16th century, but not commonly adopted till the 18th.

2. Hammer-beam roofs.

These were introduced in the Perpendicular period and formed one of the finest features of that style. The term "hammer-beam" is rather

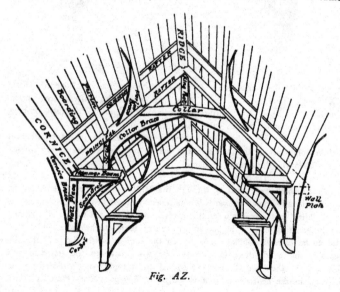

Fig. AZ.

meaningless, but it has now become universal. Fig. AZ will explain the roof better than a long description. Reference may also be made to Plate XXIV. Plate III. shews a good example of a double hammer-beam roof.

3. Collar-braced roofs.

These are a simplification of the last kind and were very common in the 15th century. In one form they were used at a much earlier date. For a late example see Plate XIII.

RUBBLE. Unsquared stone, as opposed to squared stone which is called ashlar.

SCOINSON ARCH. The inner arch of a doorway or window. It is often larger than the outer arch and of a different shape.

SEDILIA. This word, which simply means "seats," is applied to the stone recessed seats often found in the south wall of a chancel.

SHINGLES. Wooden tiles, used especially on spires.

SPANDREL. The space included in a triangle which has one curved and two straight sides.

SPLAY. The widening of an opening by slanting its sides. A window often has a narrow outer arch, and a wide inner arch: it is then said to be splayed.

SQUINT or HAGIOSCOPE. An opening in the wall of a church to give a view of an altar.

STANDARD. The upright end of a seat, often carved with poppy-heads and other ornaments.

STOUP or STOCK. A stone basin for holy water, often seen within a niche near the principal doorway of a church.

STRING-COURSE. A projecting course of moulded stone, generally horizontal. It is frequently continued from a hood-moulding or an abacus. Its mouldings are very similar to those of an abacus (Figs. A to I). In addition to the forms illustrated, the semi-hexagonal string-course is very common in the Norman period. In the Perpendicular style string-courses and hood-mouldings are frequently undercut with a broad and shallow hollow.

STRUT. A piece of wood in compression, as opposed to a tie-beam which is in tension. A slanting strut is shown in Fig. AY, and an upright strut in Fig. AZ.

TIE-BEAM. See ROOF.

TRACERY. See WINDOW.

TRANSITION. See GOTHIC.

TRANSOM. A horizontal bar in a window. It is sometimes seen in the Decorated period, but is far more common in the Perpendicular, especially in the latter part.

TREFOIL. See WINDOW.

TRUSS. See ROOF.

TUDOR ROSE. See ORNAMENT.

TYMPANUM. This term has several meanings. It is commonly applied to the stonework between the arch of a Norman doorway and the line of its supporting imposts (Plate XXXVI.).

VAULT. An arched stone roof. The simplest form, familiar in railway tunnels, is called a barrel or waggon vault. A groined vault is formed by the intersection of two barrel vaults at right angles. Fan or conoidal vaults are a beautiful development of the Perpendicular period. There is hardly any vaulting in the churches of Shropshire, but a splendid example of fan vaulting may be seen at Tong (Plate IX.).

VOLUTE. A spiral ornament derived from Ionic capitals (Plate XLI.). It is often used in Norman work (Fig. 25).

WINDOW. Norman windows are generally round-headed. They are small in the early part of the period, but usually much larger later on. Most Early English windows are lancets. When three are placed together, the middle one is generally higher than the others (Plate XXIV.): the arrangement shewn in Plate XXVI. is very unusual. Tracery originated in placing two or three lancets under one hood-moulding and piercing the enclosed stonework. When the holes are few, the tracery is called "plate tracery"; but, when the holes become numerous and the dividing stonework is narrowed down, the term employed is "bar tracery," for the appearance is that of a bar of some flexible substance twisted about, and not of a pierced plate. Plate tracery is an Early English sign. Bar tracery developed out of it late in the 13th century. All plate tracery is geometrical. Bar tracery in the Decorated period is geometrical or curvilinear. Geometrical tracery can be readily drawn with compasses and consists

Fig. BA.   Fig. BB.   Fig. BC.

largely of trefoils (Fig. BA), quatrefoils (Fig. BB), cinquefoils, sexfoils, and multifoils. Curvilinear tracery also uses quatrefoils, etc., but they are

of a kind not readily drawn with compasses (Fig. BC). Speaking
generally, geometrical tracery was used in the first half of the Decorated
period and gave way gradually to curvilinear tracery for the remainder
of the period. For geometrical tracery see Plates III., IV., XII., XXIII.,
XLII., XLVII. Curvilinear tracery is shewn in Plates XXVII.,
XXXVII. (side windows), XLV. A variety of the latter, called
reticulated tracery from its net-like appearance, is illustrated in Plates
XIV., XV., XLV. Flamboyant tracery, so called from its flame or
torch-like appearance, is not uncommon on woodwork. There is a little
on the screen at Lydbury North (Plate XLVIII.). The Flamboyant style
in France corresponds roughly in date with the Perpendicular style
in England. Cusps are the curved projections under arches (Plate
XXXIX.): they were introduced towards the end of the 13th, and used
all through the 14th and 15th centuries. In the 16th century they are
often omitted. The absence of the cusp is therefore a very early or a
very late sign. Perpendicular tracery, as its name implies, consists
largely of perpendicular lines. The lower part of all traceried windows
has these, but, in the Perpendicular period, the upper part consists
mainly of vertical lines instead of geometrical or curvilinear. For
examples, see Plates II., IV., V., X., XI., XVII., XXI., XXIX.

The characteristic tracery of the various periods is often
seen on screens, roofs, etc., as well as in windows.

The Hundred

of

Brimstree.

Albrighton.

St. Mary.

THIS church consists of nave and aisles; chancel, with vestry and organ chamber on the north side; tower at the west end; and south porch.

There is a mention of a certain Nicholas, priest of Albrighton in 1186-7, and part of the present church is probably of that date, namely, the lower portion of the tower, which is Transitional in character.

The late Norman church presumably consisted of nave and chancel, besides the western tower.

About the middle of the 13th century the height of the tower was increased, the work being very similar to the tower at Shiffnal of the same style. The south aisle, which was rebuilt in 1853, seems to have been of the same period, so far as can be determined from old drawings.

In the 14th century the chancel was built or rebuilt.

There were some slight alterations in the Perpendicular period, and in modern times a north aisle has been added, the south aisle rebuilt, and other changes made.

THE CHANCEL

is of the 14th century, if we may judge from the windows, which are, of course, Decorated. The chancel arch is modern and does not help us in determining the date.

The fine east window is unusually large for the size of the wall: the transom is not at all a common feature in Decorated windows. The smaller window on the south side is a simple composition, but the other one is a fine example with reticulated tracery. There is a blocked window, no doubt of the same period, on the north side. I cannot say what the recess below was used for; it does not look like an aumbry. The work is modern, but the four-centred arch is presumably copied, and shews the period to be Perpendicular, probably of the same date as the vestry. The sedilia and piscina on the south side are of the same character. The latter is peculiar: the basin is partly supported by a corbel, with Perpendicular mouldings; over this is an ogee canopy, surmounted again by a shelf and a four-centred arch. The stone-work of the piscina and sedilia has been partly renewed, but the old form is, I suppose, preserved. The graceful collar-roof appears to be original, though it was repaired at the restoration.

There are two interesting tombs. That on the south side is supposed to commemorate the only Duke of Shrewsbury, who died in 1718 and was buried in this church: it has a rude cross and other ornamentation.

The northern tomb is of the date 1555, and is to the memory of Sir John Talbot de Grafton and Frances his wife, as the inscription reveals. The armour is interesting, as shewing the transition from the Early Tudor to the Elizabethan period. We have the mail skirt, pauldrons, pass-guards, and tuilles of the Early Tudor, but the approach of the Elizabethan style is shewn by the ruffs, now small, at the neck and wrists. The SS. collar is worn. The female figure has ruffs at the wrists and the Mary Queen of Scots cap. The figures below present similar characteristics, and the architectural ornament is more Classical than Gothic.*

The upper figures have suffered sadly from the contemptible vandals, who seek to immortalise their unworthy selves by defacing the monuments of others. The dates shew that this vice is not confined to the 19th century, or the 18th.

The interior arrangement of the vestry and organ chamber appears to have been altered of late years, but the outer walls are old, and with their two windows, one of very curious design, belong, I should think, to the Perpendicular period.

THE NAVE

as we now see it is almost entirely modern. The north aisle was built in 1853, and the south aisle rebuilt at the same time: the old aisle had three lancets, surmounted by a quatrefoil, in the east wall, and a traceried window in the west. From these we should suppose the aisle to be of the middle of the 13th century, but it is difficult to determine, now that it has been rebuilt.

The pulpit and a chair in the vestry are of Elizabethan character.

The tower wall shews the marks of the pitch of former roofs. The blocked window is of the end of the 12th century, shewing Transitional marks— the round arch of the Norman, and the round and undercut abacus and detached shaft of the Early English.

The font is modern.

---

* See description of armour under Tong.

THE TOWER

is of two different periods, as is clearly shown by the character of the masonry.

The lower part is a curious mixture of Norman and Early English design. There are two plain round headed windows, and one, similar to the blocked window inside. Below these are acute lancets, and, on the south side, a roll and fillet hood-moulding and string-course. The buttresses are broad, of late Norman character, but have projections of Early English form, both evidently being built at the same time, and finished with a good basement moulding. There was formerly a door on the south side.

The upper part has broad lancets and small circular windows: from the resemblance to Shiffnal, one is inclined to date it back to the latter part of the Early English period.

The porch is modern.

There is a blocked door on the south side of the chancel: above are carvings of two quaint heads, of uncertain date. The hood-mouldings of the windows are not of the usual Decorated form, but the corner buttresses are diagonal, as we should expect.

Against the east wall of the south aisle is an incised slab, to the memory of Leonard Smallpece, Esquire, 1610: the broad Stuart collar is represented on the figure.

Near to this is a most remarkable tomb, clearly of Early English date, with a trefoil-headed arcade and fleurs-de-lis. There are coats of arms of several families, but it is not known to whose memory the tomb was erected. It was exhumed when the church was restored in 1853: the tomb is not mentioned by two writers, Sandford and Johnson, who refer to this church some two hundred years ago; but Johnson distinctly speaks of a marble tomb in the south aisle, which cannot now be found. This may have commemorated George, 9th Earl of Shrewsbury, who was buried here in 1630. Other members of the Talbot family were also interred at this church.

The churchyard cross has been restored; it is not unlike that at Donington, with the cable moulding, and faces at the corners of the steps.

The register of this parish dates back to 1555.

Boningale.

St. Chad.

BONINGALE is an ancient chapelry of the parish of Stockton, but has been separated from it in recent times. There seems to be a reference to the chapel in a document dated 1291, but the architectural evidence shews that the foundation is much older than this. It is a small church consisting of nave and south aisle; chancel, with a vestry on the north side; and a wooden bell-turret at the west end.

The earliest work is Norman, as appears from the round window in the nave and the remains of another window on the north side of the chancel. This latter window was evidently blocked when the vestry was added; it now has a square head on the inside, but the Norman character is well seen on the outside. The door on the south side of the chancel may also be of the same date, but it may possibly belong to the Renaissance period.

There are apparently no remains of the Early English period, but of the Decorated style we have the east window with its tracery, plain mullion, and un-hollowed hood-moulding on the outside. The small turret and spire are decorated with carvings of quatrefoils.

There are several remains of the Perpendicular period, such as the two south windows of the chancel, which are square-headed. The panelled roofs of the nave and chancel are worthy of notice. The nave roof has carvings of angels, and other ornaments. The vestry seems to have been added in the 16th century; for the square-headed windows are of a late form, and the arch between the vestry and the chancel is round. The communion table and pulpit are Elizabethan or rather later.

Considerable alterations have taken place in modern times. The west wall and door have been rebuilt, windows restored on the north side of the nave, and a south aisle with carved columns added to the church. The carved font is also modern. The restoration took place in 1861.

There is a cross in the churchyard, converted in modern times into a sun-dial.

There is an ancient chalice of good design: the paten, which fits on to the top, has the date 1579. The register dates back to 1698.

Bridgnorth.

St. Leonard.

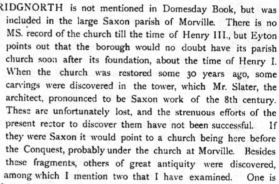

BRIDGNORTH is not mentioned in Domesday Book, but was included in the large Saxon parish of Morville. There is no MS. record of the church till the time of Henry III., but Eyton points out that the borough would no doubt have its parish church soon after its foundation, about the time of Henry I. When the church was restored some 30 years ago, some carvings were discovered in the tower, which Mr. Slater, the architect, pronounced to be Saxon work of the 8th century. These are unfortunately lost, and the strenuous efforts of the present rector to discover them have not been successful. If they were Saxon it would point to a church being here before the Conquest, probably under the church at Morville. Besides these fragments, others of great antiquity were discovered, among which I mention two that I have examined. One is the ornament of round interlacing arches now built into the belfry, and the other a square capital, with carvings of volutes and rude foliage. Both these shew late Norman characteristics, and we may safely conclude that the church was built or added to towards the end of the 12th century. Another fragment seems to be a corbel, with the mask ornament, and is therefore probably of the 13th century, though possibly of the 14th.

As regards the present building, I have given reasons farther on for thinking that the chancel is of the 13th century, or late in the 12th, and the arch at the west of the south aisle is probably of the same period: the Norman fragments, already referred to, may be contemporary. Assuming these conclusions to be correct, we seem to have evidence that the Transitional church consisted of at least chancel, nave, south aisle and possibly tower at the end of the south aisle. However, with the little MS. evidence, and the scanty architectural remains, it is impossible to construct a complete architectural history of the church, and some of the foregoing is necessarily conjectural.

In the 14th century, one or more chantries were founded here. An indication of a chantry existed some 40 years ago, in the form of a piscina, in the south aisle: this has now disappeared, and I cannot therefore say whether it belonged to a 14th century chapel.   No part of the present building can be proved to be of this date.

A lofty tower was built south of the church in 1468, and to the same period belong the battlement and string-course on the chancel, noticed farther on.

John Leland visited the church in 1536, and described it as "a very fayre one," and the only parish church in the town.

Some of the roofs appear to have been constructed early in the 17th century.

In 1645, an officer in Charles I.'s army, named Symonds, writes of the church as "a noble structure," ornamented with painted windows.   A sketch he made of one of these shews us a knight clad in mail of the Surcoat period, of the latter part of the 13th century—further evidence of the existence of a church at that time.   Symonds also mentions some altar tombs in the north aisle.

An encounter took place on March 31st, 1646, in the churchyard, between the Royalist and Parliamentary troops.   Much damage was then done to the church, and, after the Restoration, Charles II. issued a proclamation to aid a collection for repairing the edifice.   The north aisle, when built we cannot say, appears to have been destroyed in 1646, and a wall built afterwards, north of the nave.   Other dilapidations were no doubt made good.

However, the church was in a deplorable condition early in this century, and restoration was commenced soon after the Rev. G. Bellett came in 1835.   The chancel was first dealt with, but it was many years before the main portion of the work was done, i.e. the erection of a new north aisle in 1860, the rebuilding of the south aisle in 1862, and the rebuilding of the tower in 1870.   The architect was Mr. Slater, of Regent Street, London.

It will be seen that most of the present edifice is modern, but there are several points of interest, which I will mention in detail.   Unfortunately, there is no exact record in the parish of the recent alterations, and it is difficult in some cases to say whether work is old or new.

THE CHANCEL

at present has a very modern appearance, there being little ancient detail.   An old print, which seems to have been made about 1850, shews an east window of early Decorated form.   If this was ancient, it would shew that the chancel is at least as old as the 14th century.   I will deal presently with the evidence outside the church.   The print also shews a chancel arch supported by octagonal columns, but one can scarcely make out what the mouldings were like.   The present arch is modern, as are all the windows.   The piscina and sedilia are modern, but may well represent the *general* form of the ancient. The restored arch on the opposite side presumably reproduces an ancient one:

it is a shouldered arch and was probably for an aumbry. The small opening on the same side was no doubt for communication to the outside of the church, but for what purpose it is now impossible to say: these windows are more commonly on the south, and not, as here, on the north side of the church. There is a small brass plate of the 18th century, and good and bad modern plates. The oak stalls, lately added, are of beautiful workmanship. There is a modern hammer-beam roof of good design: the corbels which support it have been thought by some to be ancient, but I think they must be modern: they are of Perpendicular form, ornamented with angels. The reredos was erected in memory of the Rev. G. Bellett, who was rector for 35 years, and mainly instrumental in restoring the church.

THE NAVE

is chiefly remarkable for its great width, 43 feet, and for the hammer-beam roof which spans it. This has often been considered to be of the time of Charles II., but it is difficult to say how much damage was done at that time, and this roof may be earlier, though of course, as its non-Gothic details shew, not before the time of Elizabeth. The west windows are modern. There is an early Jacobean chest in the south-east corner. The pulpit is modern. The peculiar blocked arch on the south helps to sustain the thrust of the tower.

THE NORTH AISLE

was rebuilt in 1860. The original aisle appears to have been destroyed in the Civil War, and the north wall rebuilt where the pillars now are. In 1862 there were marks in this wall shewing that the aisle originally extended all along the nave, with the exception of about ten feet at the west. It may have consisted of chapels, and not have been an ordinary aisle to the nave. At the restoration in 1860, the wall which then bounded the nave on this side was removed, the present columns erected, and the north wall built in its present position; whether this latter is on the original foundations or not I have been unable to discover. The roof is curious: the highly carved brackets are evidently modern, but the upper part looks old, perhaps of the 17th century: if this is so, I cannot say where the roof was brought from, for the aisle was non-existent 40 years ago.

THE SOUTH AISLE

was rebuilt in 1862. The arch on the west side is, however, ancient, and might have been built at any time from the end of the 12th century onwards. The position of the arch, north and south, is peculiar, and suggests that it may have been the entrance from the south aisle to an older tower, which, perhaps, communicated with the church only in this way. The detail on the capitals and bases is, of course, modern, but on one of the capitals near is some very quaint carving, which may be old. The roofs of the aisle appear to be Elizabethan or early Jacobean. Like the nave roof they are of the hammer-beam form, but the brackets are different. There are some very quaint monumental slabs of iron against the south wall. Here, too, is the sword of Colonel Billingsley, the commander of the Royalist troops, who fell in the churchyard on March 31st, 1646. The font was presented to the church in 1862. It appears to be of the 15th century, but nothing is known of its history.

THE TOWER

was almost entirely rebuilt in 1870, in the same style as the old one, which dated from the year 1468. It is a fine massive structure, and must be a landmark for miles round. Its position, directly south of the church, certainly adds to the general effect. In the belfry are the Norman carvings of interlaced arches already referred to, built into the wall.

THE EXTERIOR

of the church is almost entirely modern. The old walls of the chancel were retained, but they have been re-faced, except on the north side, where portions of the old stone-work can be seen. The basement moulding is most interesting, and has several old stones. The semi-hexagonal string-course is a common Norman form, but the double slope below is rather a later sign. It seems to me quite possible that the basement may be of the end of the 12th century, though the 13th may be more probable, bearing in mind the character of the plain stone-work. This moulding is a most important piece of evidence, and proves that the chancel is ancient, and, as mentioned before, it seems to me *possible* that this wall, the arch across the south aisle, and the Norman fragments, may have been erected at the same time. High up on this north wall can be seen a few stones of the old battlement and string-course. These are Perpendicular, the battlement being moulded vertically as well as horizontally, and the string-course being a common form in the 15th century.

An octagonal building has been erected on the north side of the chancel as a library. It contains a chair of early Jacobean character, which belonged to Bishop Heber. A decayed metal chalice and paten are also preserved here. They were found in the hands of a skeleton, buried in the monastery of the Grey Friars, and are probably of the 13th century. Most of the sacramental plate belonging to the church is modern, but there is a flagon of some interest, as it dates from the latter part of the Commonwealth. There is an ancient stone coffin near the tower. Till the restoration in 1862, a dormer window to the south aisle existed ; this was probably erected in the time of Charles II.

The parish register dates from 1551. Richard Baxter commenced his ministry here.

Bridgnorth.

St. Mary Magdalene.

HIS church has a somewhat remarkable history, though the present structure is only 100 years old. The great Roger De Montgomery built a castle and endowed a collegiate church at Quatford. His son, Robert De Belesme, removed both to Bridgnorth at the end of the 11th century, or the beginning of the 12th. The church was really the chapel of the castle, and built within its precincts. It was also a collegiate church, with a dean and five prebendaries. When the castle passed into the hands of Henry I., the whole patronage was vested in the Crown, and St. Mary Magdalene's church became a Royal Free Chapel. Till quite recently it constituted, with some surrounding parishes, the Royal Peculiar of Bridgnorth, exempt from ordinary episcopal jurisdiction. It was not a parish church before the time of Edward III., and probably not till the 17th century. Leland speaks of St. Leonard's as the only parish church in 1536. The collegiate body do not appear to have performed their work very regularly, for we find that Henry III. founded a new chapel, appointing a chaplain to conduct services. However, the dean and prebendaries were continued, and it is interesting to note that the prebendal stall of Alveley was held in 1360 by William of Wykeham, who, of course, had the greatest influence on English architecture, in introducing the Perpendicular style at Winchester and Oxford.

Very little evidence seems to remain to show the date of the building which preceded the present church. An old print, copied in Bellett's *Antiquities of Bridgnorth*, shews the church with nave, long chancel, and western tower. There appears to be Norman work on the south side of the nave, but the drawing is not accurate enough to decide, and we are left to conjecture how much, if any, of the building belonged to the time of Robert De Belesme, or to that of Henry III.

The old church, being dilapidated, was taken down in 1792, and the present Grecian edifice erected in its place. Telford was the architect, and the church was rebuilt on the same site, but facing north and south. It has a tower at the north end, and the nave is divided from the aisles by twelve Ionic columns. A square recess, at the south end, was replaced in 1876 by an apsidal chancel, designed by Sir Arthur Blomfield.

The communion plate is modern. The register goes back to 1610.

Claverley.

All Saints.

THIS CHURCH was connected with the collegiate foundation, endowed by Roger De Montgomery at Quatford, and afterwards transferred by Robert De Belesme to Bridgnorth. It appears that the Dean of Bridgnorth was also Rector of Claverley. The church, as it now stands, is extremely puzzling from an architectural point of view, and the following notice has taken many hours of thought and care to compile. The unrestored state of the building, at any rate, has this advantage, that the difficulties are not increased by the modern alterations and falsifications of history that one sometimes meets with.

The earliest part of the church is the arcade on the north side of the nave, which, from its plain and massive Norman character, may belong to the time of Roger de Montgomery,—*i.e.*—the latter part of the 11th century. However, there is nothing to show that it is not some years later; indeed, when we examine the Norman tower, we are led to think that it, and presumably the north arcade also, was built well on into the 12th century. There would probably be a Saxon church in Earl Roger's time, and it would be this that he would associate with his collegiate body at Quatford. The Norman church must have consisted of nave, north aisle, and tower south of the nave; there would probably be a chancel as well, but there are no remains of it now.

In the latter part of the 13th century, the south aisle was built, making the west side of the tower no longer external, and necessitating either then, or at some later period, an arch connecting the aisle with the tower. The west window of the nave was put up at the same time, and the west wall rebuilt.

Later on in the Decorated period, a large chancel was built, and a vestry on the north side of it; the latter has since disappeared. Two windows were also inserted in the tower, one looking south, and the other east.

In the Perpendicular period, the north aisle, but not the arcade separating it from the nave, was rebuilt. About the same time, a

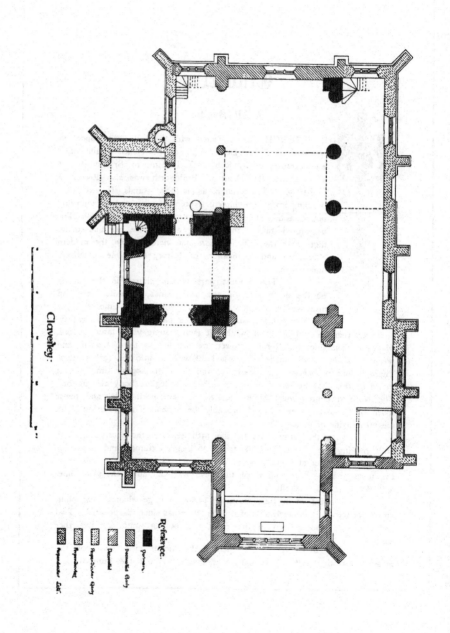

Claverley.

chapel was erected on the north side of the chancel, the former west wall of the vestry becoming the east wall of the chapel; two arches connected the chapel and chancel, necessitating the removal to the new north wall of two Decorated windows. Later on in the 15th century, the height of the tower was about doubled, the porch and clerestory added, the roof of the nave probably erected, and the south wall of the south aisle rebuilt. Later still, perhaps early in the 16th century, a chapel was built on the *south* of the chancel, connected with it by a wide arch. This chapel made the *east* wall of the tower no longer external, and necessitated an arch on that side. Besides this, the north arch of the tower, probably Norman till that time, was replaced by a Perpendicular one.

The next date seems to be 1601, when the chancel roof was erected.

In the 18th century, some of the roofs were renewed, and a great quantity of woodwork carved, and finally some alterations were made in 1832.

I will now describe the church in detail, and give the evidence on which the foregoing history has been constructed.

THE CHANCEL

was built in the 14th century, as the various details shew. The east window is very large and fine; on either side are windows of rather peculiar design, the straight lines shewing the approach of the Perpendicular style, but still the windows are quite Decorated, as will be shewn later on. On the north side is a blocked door, which I will refer to when dealing with the exterior. There are three sedilia, and a piscina with plain unhollowed hood-mouldings: that over the piscina has a finial in the form of a cross. The roof looks like a Jacobean design, and the period is the end of the reign of Elizabeth. The date, 1601, is on one bracket, and there are various devices on others: one has the Gatacre coat of arms. The brackets are very ornate, and one would think the hidden part of the roof was good, but I am told there is no special interest about it. The chancel arch has Decorated mouldings, a double course of a poor sunk quarter round following the arch, and the abaci having the scroll: unfortunately the bases cannot be seen. There is a carved panel on the north pillar. The west window can be better observed from the outside, and I will refer to it later. The buttress against the tower was no doubt added at the time the tower was raised, or later. The clerestory was a Perpendicular addition: the windows are in pairs, an unusual feature: they have had cusps, remains of which can be seen.

THE WOOD-WORK.

There is a great deal of this scattered about the church, and it

will be convenient to deal with it under one heading.   At first one is very
much puzzled by the appearance of the carved wood, for most of it is of
Gothic design, and yet one finds it used to ornament the galleries.   It would
seem as if a screen, part of which is in the north aisle, had been broken up,
and used in modern times to ornament the pulpit, reading desks, pews, and
galleries.   But, on carefully examining the fragments scattered about, one
must come to the conclusion that none of them are really old: the carving,
though fair in parts, is not genuine Gothic, and the wood used is very common
stuff.   The date on the pulpit is 1715, and the best explanation of this
pseudo-Gothic work seems to be that it was all carved in the 18th century.
That all knowledge of mediæval forms had not died out at that time is proved
by the carvings on the roof of the north aisle, dated 1706, and a bracket to
the nave roof, which also has an 18th century date.   It would appear as if
all the ornamental carving on the pulpit, reading desks, pews, and galleries
was executed by one man.   His knowledge of ancient work was remarkable
for that period, and he could carve Elizabethan or Gothic forms at will!
With the former he adorned (?) the pulpit and sounding board, and with the
latter the galleries, pews, and desks.   This is not a far-fetched idea, for the
roof of the north aisle shews the same mixture.   I do not suppose that all
his carving is in its original position, *e.g.*—the screen in the north aisle, for
a board on the tower tells us of changes made in 1832, when "altering and
erecting galleries" took place.   In these remarks I am not referring to some
dark-coloured pews in the north chapel, to an old chest in the south chapel,
to the chancel roof, or to the nave roof; the last mentioned I think must be real
Perpendicular work, and only repaired in the 18th century.   I should not
have entered into the matter at such length, but for the fact that the appearance
of this wood-work is very deceptive.

THE NORTH AISLE

was rebuilt in the Perpendicular period, but the evidence of this, and the
windows, can be better observed from the outside: two of these have fragments
of 15th century glass remaining.   The Norman arches are simply recessed
without chamfers: the columns are very massive and have round abaci, which,
though an exception to the rule, is not very uncommon on large pillars at
this period.   There is a puzzle here which I have not yet been able to solve;
it is this.   On the north side of the arcade, at its extreme east and west
limits, are two projecting pieces of stone, rather higher than the top of the
abaci.   The detail of the one at the west is obscured by the whitewash, but
that at the east presents distinctly Norman characteristics.   The question is,
what were these stones for?   They cannot have been for a flat roof at this
height, and they do not look massive enough to have supported a vault.   The

similarity of the two in position and form precludes the idea that they were built in at a later period.

The eastern arch of the arcade is pointed, and was no doubt added later : the next pillar has the same character as the western respond, *but the Norman aisle cannot have ended there*, for, not only would it not fit in with the position of the tower opposite, but the Norman stone already referred to, farther east, shews that the aisle extended at least as far as that. This eastern arch is narrower than the others : there cannot have been a round arch here, unless it was lower than the others, which is unlikely, and we must suppose that there was a wall, and that the aisle was shut off to that extent from the nave, perhaps for a chapel. It is now impossible to say when the wall was removed, and the present poor arch substituted. The niche in the eastern respond is of very nondescript character.

Here are the remains of the screen already referred to, and a slab commemorating Richard Spicer, merchant ; it is partly under the pews, but the date has been made out to be 1408. This part was called the Spicer chapel, and afterwards the Crowther chapel.

THE NORTH CHAPEL.

Puzzling features are seen in this chapel as elsewhere. We find a Perpendicular chapel with Decorated windows, but these were evidently removed from the old wall of the chancel, when its place was taken by the two arches. For we have clear evidence that the chapel is later than the Decorated chancel. The mouldings of the arches are Perpendicular, a wave moulding being used, with wide concave parts, and the bases of the pillars being distinctly of the bell-shaped form. But there are other indications. There is a buttress of Decorated character in the south-west corner, no doubt erected to help to sustain the thrust of the wide chancel arch : besides this, we see, east of the arches, a slope at the bottom of the wall, shewing clearly that this was an *external* wall in the Decorated period. A remarkable fact is that the slope is continued along the *east* wall, but I must reserve the discussion of this point till later.

The ornaments on the vestry partition are indeed pseudo-Gothic : whether they were erected in 1715 or 1832, it is perhaps hardly worth while to enquire.

The chapel belongs to the Gatacre family : it is connected with the north aisle by a very poor arch—post-reformation probably, as there would no doubt be an eastern altar in the Spicer chapel.

THE SOUTH AISLE

appears to have been built late in the 13th century, the two arches which separate it from the nave being evidently of that period. The heads and animals are most curious (see Plate I.), but it is the foliage, which marks the date. It is neither the "stiff leaf" of the Early English, nor the natural of the Decorated, but partakes of both characteristics : this is specially shewn on the middle pillars ; the bases cannot be seen, but are probably similar to those in the nave at Shiffnal.

The font is a very interesting example of Norman work (see Plate I.). The upper part has carvings of conventional foliage, and underneath is a round arched arcade, with very peculiar notched columns : a row of beads is below this, and a heavy roll underneath. I will refer to the windows and the west wall of the tower later on. The view in Eyton's *Antiquities* shews the carving on the pillars more clearly than it can now be seen, and it seems as if the whitewash must have been put on since that view was taken. The font was covered as well, but the present vicar had it cleaned and the carving revealed.

THE SOUTH CHAPEL

was built late in the Perpendicular period. It is connected with the chancel by a wide arch with coarse mouldings, but the remains of Decorated hood-mouldings above, and a string-course on either side, shew very clearly that the chapel is an addition of a later period. All the windows are Perpendicular, of poor execution, and the glass is modern. There is a piscina in the south wall, but no remains of the drain : the ornamental stone now in the piscina is of no interest or great antiquity. The east wall of the tower I will refer to presently. The roof is nothing less than a sham.

This Chapel belongs to the Gatacre family, as well as the one on the north side opposite. There are two slabs on the east wall : the one on the right is the earlier, and commemorates William Gatacre, Esquire, who died in 1577, and his wife : the other is to Francis Gatacre, who died in 1599, and his wife. There are two or three points of interest in these slabs, shewing the transition from mediæval to modern times. The earlier tomb has old English lettering, the later, Roman capitals : the inscription on one is in Latin, on the other in English : William Gatacre has armour, Francis is in civilian costume : all the figures have ruffs of Elizabethan character.

There is a very elaborate tomb on the south side to Sir Robert Broke, who was common serjeant and recorder of London, and speaker of the House of Commons. Sir Robert is dressed in legal costume, and wears the SS. collar (see under *Tong*). The other figures are of his two wives, the second being Dorothy Gatacre. She is represented on Sir Robert's right, and wears a beautiful pedimental head-dress : the other figure has a Mary Queen of Scots cap. The knight was the father of 17 children, who are represented below, with the wife of the first : one of the figures is wrapped in a shroud, the meaning being evident. The arms of Sir Robert and his wives are given, and

The Font.
CLAVERLEY.

the architectural ornaments are classical, the date being 1558.

THE TOWER.

I must now deal with the tower, both externally and internally, which has quite a history of its own.

The lower part is certainly Norman, as is shewn by the buttresses on the south and east sides, and the upper round windows. These latter may not look decisive from the outside, but the splays on the inside are very clear. The basement moulding on the south side has a semi-hexagonal string-course, and a slope below: remains of this can be seen on the west side (see Plate I.), and of the string-course on the east. The puzzling thing at first is that a Norman tower should be supported by three arches of later period, but the explanation is not far to seek. The Norman tower must have had three outside walls, as their basement moulding shews: it stood south of the nave, apparently at the extreme east of it.

The building of the south aisle, at the end of the 13th century, necessitated the introduction of an arch to connect it with the tower. This arch is of a nondescript character, and might have been erected at almost any time: it is round on one side and pointed on the other, and breaks into the Norman moulding (see Plate I.).

The next change in the building was at a later time in the Decorated period, when the south window was inserted, and also one on the east side, the remains of which can still be seen.

In the 15th century came the greatest change of all: the tower was almost doubled in height. Buttresses were added to the Norman ones and carried to a great height: one large buttress is inside the nave, but the form is so clumsy that it may be a much later addition for increased strength. The large upper windows do not appear to have been filled with tracery: a small window on the north side was made, rather higher up than the Norman windows on the east and west. Above the windows is a row of carved foils, and the tower is finished with a battlement, moulded vertically and horizontally, and eight pinnacles (see Plate II.).

At a later time in the Perpendicular period, the erection of the south chapel had an effect on the tower. The east wall, up to now, had been external: it now became internal, and only one external wall was left. A connection was thus required between chapel and tower, and a four-centred arch (see Plate I.) was erected, cutting into the Decorated window. This arch has very coarse mouldings, the prominent one being a wide double ogee of Perpendicular form: the hollowed hood-moulding on the east side terminates in heads, and on the west are angels, since decapitated, one of them bearing the Gatacre arms. Up to this time there had probably been a Norman arch on the north side: this was now replaced by a rough Perpendicular arch of similar character to that which divides the chancel from the south chapel.

Over both the tower arches of this period can be seen relieving arches. It would appear that the floor of the belfry was lowered at the same time, partly blocking the Decorated window on the south.

The history of the tower is so complicated that it has been necessary to write as much about it as would fully describe many another church.

THE PORCH

is an erection of the 15th century. The inner door has a heavy roll moulding, and seems to be of the same period as the south aisle, i.e.—early Decorated. The stone seats remain. There are four springs for a groined roof, at the corners, but whether the vaulting was ever carried out or not it seems difficult to say: the present roof may be as late as some of the other wood-work in the church, i.e.—the 18th century. To the same period, I suppose, belongs the painting of the Commandments, with grotesque figures of Moses and Aaron.

There is a parvise above, reached by a stair-case from the south aisle, but it has no particular interest.

THE EXTERIOR

shews variety indeed! There are steep roofs and flat roofs, and at least eight different kinds of buttresses, five sorts of battlements, and thirteen types of windows.

Leaving the church by the porch, we notice the hollowed hood-moulding above the door, and the square-headed window surmounted by a string-course, with shields. The Norman basement moulding on the tower is a great contrast to the bell-shaped Perpendicular one going round the south chapel. The windows of the chapel are very poor, and wonderfully like some at Shiffnal: the buttresses have less projection than breadth, as is not unusual in *late* Perpendicular: the gargoyles and corbels are very hideous, and badly carved: the battlement is moulded all round and has pinnacles. There is a peculiar problem suggested by some marks in the east wall of the chapel. The Decorated string-course and basement moulding of the chancel is continued a little way along the wall, and a line in the masonry seems to indicate that a small portion of this wall is more ancient than the rest. However, we have conclusive proof inside the church that this wall is later than that of the chancel, but some of the old stones and mouldings, displaced by the arch separating the chancel from the chapel, must have been used up in the later work. The problem is similar, though not the same, as that which besets us at Shiffnal in this position. As already mentioned, the north and south windows of the chancel are almost Perpendicular in their tracery, but the

CLAVERLEY.

Decorated character is shewn in the unhollowed mullions and dripstones. The east window (see Plate II.) has very fine tracery: the hood-moulding, both bulging and under-cut, is of a late Decorated form. The buttresses near are placed diagonally.

On the north side of the chancel is another peculiarity. What is the reason that the string-course and basement moulding (see Plan) stop so abruptly? It will be noticed that there is a blocked door to the chancel, which evidently led into a vestry with low roof. This seems to have been erected at the same time as the chancel, for the north window is made short to suit it: it is interesting to note that this vestry was existing when the north chapel was built, for the east window of *that* is also short: we cannot say when the vestry disappeared, but its mark is clearly left. It may be remembered that there was a basement moulding on the west side of the wall which is now the east wall of the north chapel: this shews that the wall was the external wall of the vestry, and, of course, built before the chapel. As we should expect, there is no basement moulding on the walls formerly included within the vestry. The east wall of the chapel has had quite a history of its own. It was internal on the east side for many years, internal on both sides for another period, and internal only on the west side since the disappearance of the vestry. On the north side of the chapel can be seen the Decorated windows, which were removed from the chancel; the buttresses are quite like Decorated ones: the upper part of the chapel is very debased work, perhaps of the 18th century. Very soon after this chapel was erected, the north aisle appears to have been rebuilt. The windows at first sight appear to be Decorated, but the mullions have hollow chamfers, and the work is evidently Perpendicular: the buttresses have slightly greater projection than breadth. The square headed doorway, with shields in the spandrels, seems to have been added later in the Perpendicular style, as it breaks into the basement moulding.

The west front has several features of interest. There was no doubt a wall in Norman times, occupying the middle part, but this was rebuilt and the wall of the south aisle added to it in the early Decorated period. The buttresses have greater breadth than projection, as we should expect in the 13th century. The west window is of the same period: at first sight it appears to have had no cusps, but the remains of them are evident. The original steep pitch of the nave roof can be seen: the upper part of the wall and the battlement were added in Perpendicular times, but later than the battlement of the north aisle. At first it would appear as if this was not so, for the most southerly piece of this latter battlement would not have fitted on to the steep-pitched roof, but close examination will shew that this particular piece is not like the rest, but is of debased character, like that on the north chapel.

The south wall of the south aisle seems to have been rebuilt at the same time the porch was erected.

I fear even the patience of an enthusiast will be exhausted by this account of Claverley church, but so many different styles are represented, and the church is so untouched by modern restoration, that it is most valuable for purposes of historical study. As before mentioned, there is great variety in buttresses, battlements, and windows, among other features. I subjoin a chronological list, for the benefit of those who wish to increase their knowledge on these points, but, of course, a visit to the church is necessary, to understand the allusions properly. The exact periods must be a matter of opinion in some cases. I have bracketed those which are of the same period, but not necessarily of the same form.

BUTTRESSES.

1.	South and east walls of tower	Norman
2.	West wall of nave	Early Decorated
3.	Chancel	} Decorated
4.	South-west corner of north chapel (interior)	
5.	North chapel	} Early Perpendicular
6.	North aisle	
7.	Tower	
8.	Porch	} Perpendicular
9.	South aisle	
10.	South chapel	Late Perpendicular
11.	North wall of tower (interior)	Debased

BATTLEMENTS.

1.	North aisle	Early Perpendicular
2.	Porch	
3.	South aisle	
4.	West front and clerestory	} Perpendicular
5.	Tower	
6.	South chapel	Late Perpendicular
7.	North chapel	} Debased
8.	One piece on west of north aisle	

WINDOWS.

1.	Tower	Norman
2.	West of nave	Early Decorated

WINDOWS.—*Continued.*

3.	East of chancel	
4.	North and south of chancel	
5.	North of north chapel	Decorated
6.	South of tower (lower)	
7.	East of tower (blocked)	
8.	East of north chapel	Early Perpendicular
9.	North aisle	
10.	Porch	
11.	South aisle	Perpendicular
12.	Clerestory	
13.	Tower	
14.	South chapel	Late Perpendicular

The cross in the churchyard (see Plate II.) is ancient, and is probably Perpendicular: it was removed many years ago from opposite the vicarage, and the shaft shortened at the same time.

The communion plate is modern. The register dates back to 1568, and has recently been very carefully indexed by the present vicar.

Donington.

Dedication unknown; probably St. Cuthbert.

THERE seems little doubt that Donington church was founded by Roger de Montgomery between 1085 and 1094, and the advowson given to the Abbey of Shrewsbury. No part of the present edifice, however, dates back to that time, and we are, as usual, obliged to ascertain the history of the fabric from the architectural evidence it supplies.

The lower part of the tower, which fell down in 1879, seems to have been built at the end of the 12th century, but the oldest part of the church, as it now stands, is the chancel, which dates from a hundred years later. The upper part of the old tower was of late Perpendicular character, and the nave was apparently rebuilt in 1635. Finally we have the restoration, very well carried out by Mr. Norton, of Old Bond Street, in 1879, when the north aisle and the porch were added. A few days before the re-opening of the church on March 25th, 1879, the tower fell down into the churchyard, and was rebuilt in the following year.

The east window is of a very early Decorated form, the mullions simply crossing one another without cusps. Hollow chamfers in the mullions are unusual at this period, and the under-cutting in the outer hood-moulding is broader than we should expect; there is, however, a similar example at Tong, over the arches of the south aisle. All the other windows are early Decorated with trefoils in the head. One of these on the south is a low side window, with part of the stone-work for securing the shutter remaining: the other part has been restored. In the north east window are some fragments of ancient glass, probably of the 15th century, and in the other window on the north side is some very good glass, clearly of the 14th century, as the good representations of leaves, acorns, etc. and the general character of the work shew.

The coats of arms are probably the same as those referred to by Francis Sandford as being in Donington church windows in 1663-4. Eyton supposes one of them to be that of Belmeis, Lord of Tong, and the other that of Belmeis of Donington. John de Belmeis was lord of the manor at the time this glass was probably made—*i.e.*, the end of the 13th century.

This family had been in possession since the time of Henry I., when the king had granted the lordship of the manor to Richard de Belmeis, Bishop of London. The rest of the glass in the chancel is modern. The piscina in the south wall is of a plain pointed form, and has the original stone shelf inside : a roll and fillet string-course, with modern additions and ornament, runs below the piscina : there is a similar one by the sedilia. The aumbry is in the north wall. The chancel arch is modern and has carvings of stiff-leaf foliage.

The nave is chiefly remarkable for the fine double hammer-beam roof of the date 1635, which appears several times : a tie beam at the west has the inscription

THOMAS TWIGG
CARPENTER 1635

The brackets are highly carved with patterns, leaves, and grotesque heads. The design of the roof is similar to those at Shiffnal but probably of later date. The windows are probably also of the 17th century : the absence of cusps is natural at that period, but the sub-arches are more acutely pointed than we should expect.

The north aisle, of good early Gothic design, is modern, having been erected in 1879. Some ancient seats of the Perpendicular period are placed here.

The font is modern, and so is the porch, a beautiful half-timbered erection.

On the south side of the nave can be seen the foundations of a small transept : this may have been taken down in 1635 when the nave was rebuilt. The hood-mouldings over the south windows and door of the chancel are of the scroll type : those on the north are the same, but all the heads are very poorly carved.

The tower is almost an exact reproduction of the one which fell down, but the new tower is three or four feet higher than the old one, and the pinnacles at the corners were omitted : the quatrefoil carving is very similar to that on Claverley church.

There are the remains of an ancient cross in the churchyard : the cable ornament has a Norman appearance, but the chamfer terminations are scarcely of that character.

The communion plate is modern. The register dates back to 1690.

Kemberton.

KEMBERTON, like Ryton, seems to have been included in the Saxon parish of Idshall, and the Vicar of Shiffnal is entitled to a pension of five shillings annually from the Rector of Kemberton.

There is no mention of a church here in Domesday Book, but we find that there must have been one before 1230, as there is record of a certain Gilbert being chaplain at that time.

Some fragments of the old church are still preserved, and are of thirteenth century character. This building was taken down *circa* 1781, and it is said that the tower was so strong that it had to be blown up with gunpowder! It was replaced by a red brick structure of ugly appearance: the east end was apsidal and the ordinary round-headed windows of the period were used. The brick tower still remains, but the main part of the church was rebuilt in 1881 in modern Gothic style. The design is much better than one often sees ; and, as in so many other Shropshire churches, the colour of the red sandstone adds much to the beauty of the building. The architect was Mr. Joseph Farmer of Kemberton. The pulpit, of marble and alabaster, is elaborately carved.

The living of this church is combined with that of Sutton Maddock, and the general appearance of the Georgian churches, which were built in both places, was very similar.

The registers date from 1659. There is an interesting chalice, and the top, used as a paten, has the date 1520 inscribed upon it.

Oakengates.

Holy Trinity.

AKENGATES is a modern parish, formed out of Shiffnal and Wombridge in 1855. The church was consecrated on January 25th of that year: it consists of chancel, nave with short aisles, diminutive south porch, and a small turret above the chancel arch. The roofs of the aisles are of the same pitch as that of the nave, from which they are continued. The building is handsome compared with the neighbouring church of Priorslee! Mr. Ewan Christian was the architect.

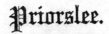

Priorslee.

St. Peter.

PRIORSLEE is an ancient chapelry of the parish of Shiffnal: it was formed into a separate parish in 1863.

From a drawing made by D. Parkes in 1816, and copied by Rev. J. Brooke, we get some idea of the old church, which was about half a mile nearer Shiffnal than the modern building. It seems to have been composed of nave, chancel, and turret, and the appearance was rather that of Norman and late Perpendicular work, but one cannot now speak with certainty.

This church was taken down, and the present brick building was erected in 1836: it consists of nave and west tower, and is about as ugly as it can be. Most of the windows are lancet shaped, but those of the tower are square-headed.

The communion plate dates from 1771, and the register from 1836.

Ryton.

Dedication unknown.

RYTON seems to have been included in the Saxon parish of Idshall, and to this day the Rector of Ryton pays an annual pension of two shillings to the Vicar of Shiffnal. The separation of the parishes probably took place in the 12th century, and we read of a certain Bernard, priest of Ryton in 1186.

No part of the present building can be proved to be of this early date, but the east and south walls of the nave seem to be ancient, particularly the thicker part of the latter at the west end.

There is record to shew that the chancel was built in 1720, but the chancel arch appears to be modern, and the vestry, all the windows, and the roof, are of recent construction. The doorway is partly original, and has a quaint head carved on the outside as a termination to the dripstone.

The roof and windows of the nave are modern, and have no great interest.

The most ornate part of the building is the north aisle, built in 1886 to the memory of William Kenyon-Slaney of Hatton Grange and Mary Slaney of Ryton Grove. The old north wall of the nave was without windows; these were inserted in 1874 and removed to their present position when the aisle was erected.

The font, which is in a peculiar position against the tower arch, is, I should think, Decorated work of the middle of the 14th century: the lower part has panelling, and the upper part quatrefoils within circles, surmounted by a sunk quarter-round moulding. The tower arch is of plain pointed character. Two corbels remain, which supported a large gallery, which was formerly carried some way up the nave.

The tower is at first sight rather puzzling, for Decorated and late Perpendicular forms are mixed. The mystery is solved when we learn from records, and from inscriptions within the tower and on one of the pinnacles, that it was built in 1710. In the debased period of Gothic architecture we constantly find tracery of Decorated rather than Perpendicular character: we are then obliged to go by the mouldings, which are here decisive; for we see that the mullions are hollow chamfered externally, and that an ogee of the

Perpendicular form is used.   We have also on the top of the tower a feeble battlement of Perpendicular character, the moulding running horizontally and vertically, pinnacles at the corners with carvings of fleurs-de-lis, and a broadly hollowed string-course below.   This kind of architecture is generally called Jacobean Gothic, but we rarely find it so late as the 18th century.   Indeed we may say that we have here at Ryton as late an example of Gothic work as can probably be found, previous to the Gothic Revival.   The doorway is modern, replacing a narrow one with a square head.

The registers date back to 1659.   The communion plate is modern.

Shiffnal.

St. Andrew.

IN very early times this parish was called Idshall or Shiffnal indiscriminately. The first instance of the word Shiffnal being used alone was in 1330, so far as we can now tell: in modern times Idshall has been almost entirely dropped, and few people are now aware that the town was ever called anything but Shiffnal.

The Saxon parish was very extensive, and included Kemberton, Ryton, Sheriffhales, and Dawley. No remains of the Saxon church, however, now exist. It was then a collegiate church, but this character ceased soon after the Conquest, when the church was made over to the abbey of St. Peter at Shrewsbury.

The present building dates from the end of the 12th century, and is most interesting from an architectural point of view, combining, as it does, examples of every period from late Norman to late Perpendicular.

The first rector, whose name we know, was William de Dunstanville, in 1188; but the Norman part of the church was probably erected some years before that time. Of that style we now have parts of the chancel, transepts, and west wall. The Norman church presumably consisted of chancel, transepts, central tower, nave and aisles, and south porch.

In the Early English period, the tower, for some reason which we cannot now fathom, was rebuilt. At the same time the old nave and aisles were swept away and new ones erected, the vaulted porch and parvise above were also built, and probably a chapel on the south side of the chancel.

In the Decorated period, the chancel was lengthened, and the magnificent east window erected. The chapel on the south side of the chancel, now called the the Moreton chapel, was erected or rebuilt later in this style.

The next great change was at the alterations to the church in 1592, after a great fire, which destroyed part of the town, besides doing considerable damage to the church. At this time the north transept appears to have been partly rebuilt, and new roofs of the nave, chancel, Moreton chapel, transepts, and south aisle, erected. However, some of the Perpendicular work in the church is probably prior to this period.

Finally, we have the restoration under Sir Gilbert Scott, completed in 1879, when the usual accretion of galleries and high pews was swept away ; the ceilings, which concealed the fine roofs, were removed, and various dilapidations made good.

I will now give a detailed description of the church, commencing with

THE CHANCEL.

The noble east window (see Plate III.) will first strike the attention ; the tracery is of a very unusual form, but the trefoils appear to have been originally cinquefoils. At the base of the window is a row of very pretty quatrefoils, beautifully moulded : the upper moulding above these quatrefoils is the scroll, as we should expect in Decorated work. On either side are two lovely windows of the same period : the mouldings of all three are very similar, the roll and fillet being used in the mullions, and a rather peculiar moulding running round the interior arches. The stained glass is of course modern, as is the glass in the other windows of the church.

The piscina and sedilia have been considerably restored, but some of the old stone remains and exhibits Decorated characteristics : the arches are cusped, and the spandrels filled in with trefoils. The chief moulding used is a heavy roll and fillet of Decorated form which is continued as a string-course ; the ornamental termination on the south side is modern.

It will be seen that all this part of the chancel, generally called the "sacrarium," is of Decorated date, *early* in the 14th century, as is shewn by the geometrical tracery and the character of the mouldings.

The Norman chancel ended where the communion rails now are. Two of the windows remain on the north side, round and deeply splayed : they are *late* in the style, as is shewn by the hood-moulding and string-course, which are composed of a broad roll, slightly undercut—a common form in the Early English style, but never occurring in *early* Norman.

There is an interesting tomb under one of these windows to Thomas Forster, vicar of the parish in 1526 : he was also prior of Wombridge and warden of Tong, and, from the coat of arms, appears to have belonged to the family of Forester, now of Willey. He wears the dress of a priest—alb, chasuble, amice, etc.,—and his feet rest against a dog. The tomb presents thoroughly Perpendicular characteristics, the four-centred arch being used, flat foliage in the spandrels, a Perpendicular battlement over the small canopies, and sham vaulting below. Without the date, too, we should know it to be *late* Perpendicular by the shallowness of the moulding, notably the feeble double ogee. The doorway next to this tomb has been restored, and looks like Early English work.

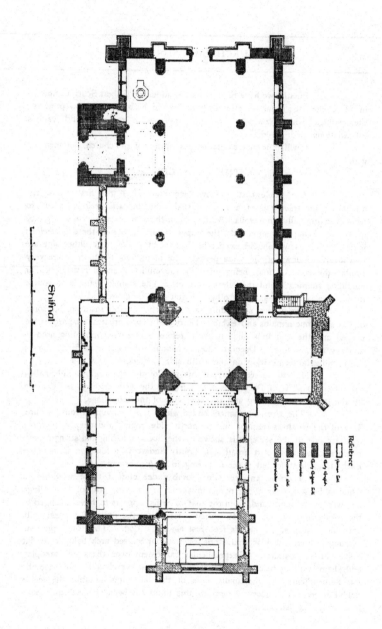

The remaining window on the north side is late Perpendicular, probably inserted in 1592: there are no cusps, and the point of the Gothic arch has almost become a round. Underneath the windows runs a modern string-course of Decorated form: I am not aware whether there was any authority for this in the old work.

The hammer-beam roof is a good example of the Elizabethan period: the supporting brackets are of distinctly Classical appearance: we have, as usual at this period, Gothic and Classical forms combined. There is some sign of an arch on the western part of the south wall. I suppose that there was formerly a Norman window here, and that the break in the masonry near is accounted for by alterations made when the Decorated arches were built.

The chancel arch is a fine specimen of Transition work: we see the Norman feeling in the square abaci, the round arch, and the general massiveness, but the approach of the Early English style is distinctly seen in the foliage on the capitals, the fillets, and above all in the beautiful tooth ornament on the west side. There is a very peculiar carving above the arch on the west. It appears to be a fruit-bearing twisted branch, coming out of the mouth of a human head: there is a large finial above. The stone seems to have decayed considerably since the view in Eyton's *Antiquities* was taken.

THE CENTRAL TOWER,

of the 13th century, is supported by four very plain arches. I have already said that we cannot now divine why the Norman tower was pulled down. In other churches, where a similar event has taken place, the original chancel arch was generally demolished: the great beauty of this example probably saved it from destruction; we can only lament that so much of the carving has disappeared. The present tower is large and imposing, but, from the width of the chancel arch and other signs, we can see that the Norman one must have been still larger, though probably not so lofty.

THE NORTH TRANSEPT

was partly rebuilt in 1592, but earlier work can be seen. On the north side are some remains of the Norman arch, which originally gave entrance to the transept, and helped to support the tower. There is also a blocked doorway, probably of the 14th century: the wave moulding used is more of the Decorated than the Perpendicular form. This door and that on the north side of the chancel apparently led to a vestry of some kind. If the door in the chancel is Early English, it follows that the vestry was built at that time, and that the door in the transept was added for greater convenience in the 14th century. Higher up on the wall are some slight remains of an arch, now blocked. I will refer to the windows later. The four-centred arch on the west is of course Perpendicular : the moulding on the east side has been renewed, but that on the west is the original : the work is good, and I think must belong to the pure Perpendicular period, a hundred years or more before the fire of 1591.

The roofs of the transepts were no doubt erected after the fire. It is remarkable that they should be flat, and those of the chancel and nave, built at the same time, high pitched. The reason, I should imagine, was that the transepts, being much more damaged by the fire than the nave and chancel, had to have their walls partly reconstructed, and the Elizabethan builders did not trouble to raise the wall to the original height, and were satisfied, as was so often the case at that period, with a very flat roof. In the chancel and nave, on the other hand, I fancy, only the roofs were destroyed, and the walls left unhurt at the old height, and therefore it was thought well to erect hammer-beam roofs. Also it must be remembered that flat roofs would have blocked part of the east and west windows. It has been suggested that the hammer-beam roofs are considerably later, perhaps by comparison with that at St. Leonard's, Bridgnorth, which may be of the time of Charles II. : but, after carefully examining the ornamental part, I cannot but think that the Elizabethan date is more likely, and it seems not improbable that, after such a serious fire, it would be necessary to reconstruct the roofs of nave and chancel. It should be mentioned that, high as is the chancel roof, it is not quite so high as the original one, as is shewn by the moulding on the tower visible outside. The nave roof was rebuilt at its original height, but the transept roofs, of course, are much lower, the old pitch being clearly visible outside. The door high up on the west wall, now blocked, communicated with the tower staircase, but one cannot now make out what it was used for.

THE SOUTH TRANSEPT.

There is more Norman work here than in the north transept. One of the old windows remains, and the string-course (restored). The arch on the east side is modern, but replaced a Norman arch of similar character, which was the entrance to a semi-circular apse, as was proved some years ago by the discovery of foundations some yards to the east. It is not at all unlikely that there was formerly an apse on the east of the *north* transept, and it is possible that there may have been one at the end of the Norman chancel. There is an aumbry on the north side of the arch, and the remains of a piscina on the south. The opening under the Norman window is of course Perpendicular : the windows I will refer to later. The roof is Elizabethan.

THE MORETON CHAPEL

takes its name from the Moreton family, which must have been of consequence in the 14th century, but is now extinct in the parish. We have no record of its foundation, and are obliged, as usual, to learn its history from the architectural features.

Of Norman work we have of course the arch which leads to the south transept. To the south of this can be seen the mark of the pointed roof of the apse, and a bit of the Norman string-course, which was formerly external.

The arches between the chapel and the chancel are finely moulded, and are late Decorated, probably about 1360. We see the Decorated form in the capitals of the two responds, which have the scroll moulding to the abaci : the centre capital has not the scroll, but the sunk quarter-round under the abacus is almost as distinctive of the style. The work is, however, *late*, as is revealed by the bases, which are almost of the bell-shaped form, and by the hood-mouldings, which are hollowed out in the Perpendicular manner. The windows are of the same date, and have *flowing* tracery, a contrast to the earlier *geometrical* tracery in the chancel. The moulding chiefly used in all four windows is a bold roll and fillet. A string-course of the same period has been cut away from the east wall, but the south wall has portions of a similar one.

But though the general character of the work is late Decorated, there are one or two indications of earlier work, which are extremely puzzling. I refer chiefly to the remains of the sedilia in the south wall. After carefully examining these, I can come to no other conclusion than that they are Early English. This places one in a great difficulty, for almost everything in the chapel,—walls, windows, arches, mouldings,—is late Decorated, but the evidence of earlier work in the sedilia, with trefoil heads and deep moulding, is so strong that I am bound to consider it decisive. The sedilia in the chancel are *early* Decorated, and yet are surely of a later form than these. But if the form is not enough, what must we think of the way the sedilia are cut into by the south east window? Surely this is sufficient proof that the window is of later date. I speak thus fully about the matter, as the Moreton chapel has always been considered to be of the 14th century, and neither the Rev. J. Brooke nor the Rev. J. L. Petit, in their accounts of the church, have dealt with this important indication of early work. There is one other piece of evidence, which can be seen on the outside of the east wall. It is the way the early Decorated string-course of the chancel is continued a little way along the wall of the chapel. There appears to be a break in the masonry near, as if a former wall had been pulled down, and been rebuilt. Do not these two signs shew that there was a wall here before the late Decorated period ? At first one would say that this was built in the early Decorated time, by the character of the string-course ; but a string-course was sometimes added at a later period. Bearing then all the evidence in mind, are we not driven to the conclusion that there was a chapel here in Early English days, occupying the same site as the present? If so, its eastern wall would have been a continuation of the end wall of the Norman chancel. It would, no doubt, have been entered by the Norman arch on the west; but, whether there were any openings to the chancel, and if so, why they were afterwards replaced in the late Decorated period, we cannot now determine. This theory may, after all, turn out to be incorrect, but I can see no other way of accounting for the sedilia of distinct Early English character.

The opening on the north side of the Norman arch contained, I suppose, the staircase to a rood loft, but this was not generally on the south side of a church, and there are no signs of the loft on the arches which support the tower.

The roof is of the hammer-beam form, and was probably erected in the Elizabethan period, at the same time as those of the chancel and nave.

There are several tombs of the Brigges family, who succeeded the Moretons at Haughton, and were ancestors of the Brookes, the present possessors. Two of these are elaborate monuments of the Elizabethan character, with the neck-ruffs and other fashions of the period. The oldest of these, 1596, is to Oliver Brigges of Ernestry Park, in the parish of Abdon. There is no ancient tomb of the Moretons, but a stone remains with most of the word Moreton carved upon it. From the form of the letters we should conclude that it is not earlier than the 17th century.

There is a carved table, dated 1634, and an old chest of 1664.

The Moreton chapel is now used as a vestry and organ chamber.

THE NAVE

consists of four bays, and is well worth study. The hammer-beam roof is probably Elizabethan, as I have already explained.

The octagonal columns, rather plain in appearance, have been considerably restored, and it is difficult to assign them to their proper date (see Fig. 1 and Plate III.). However, I think it is tolerably certain that they belong to the latter part of the Early English period, say about 1250. Early English they are, as we see by the undercut abacus; but the Decorated style is evidently approaching, for the hood-mouldings are of a form which is more common then than in Early English, and above all, as anyone with a good knowledge of mouldings will allow, the date is shewn by the character of the bases, where the lowest member *has a flat edge underneath*. The west window (now restored) quite fits in to this theory, being of a late Early English form, the sub-arches of the tracery having no cusps.

Fig 1:

PLATE III.

SHIFFNAL.

THE NORTH AISLE

was rebuilt at the recent restoration, and new windows inserted: the former ones were square-headed and had wooden frames. The hood-mouldings over the arches are the same as those on the south side, but all the heads on both sides of the arcade have been renewed: some of the original ones remain on the south arcade.

THE SOUTH AISLE,

in the part west of the porch, is Early English, with modern windows and roof. East of the porch, we find that the aisle was widened in late Perpendicular days: the windows were formerly of this type, but have been renewed in a slightly different form.

The position of the Norman south wall is fixed by the west window of the transept, and the string-course, which were of course external. The original slope of the roof can also be seen, and, possibly, part of the original wall on the north side, east of the arcade. The Norman window (see Plate III.) is the most striking object in the aisle: that it is late in the style we know by the undercut hood-moulding and the banded shafts. Something very like a Norman buttress is seen against the east wall of the porch: if this is so, it seems to shew that there was a Norman porch, buttressed on the east side. However, this was somewhat altered at the restoration, and one cannot speak decisively.

The roof is probably Elizabethan, the ornamental carving being of a very late Gothic form, with traces of Classical work.

The font is modern.

THE PORCH

is a beautiful specimen of Early English work. There are two compartments, one inside the church, and both are vaulted in the early groined manner, with finely moulded ribs and carved "stiff-leaf" bosses. The parvise above is by no means common so early as the 13th century: it was probably used first as a priest's room, and afterwards for a school. The present roof is modern, and so are the rails on the east side: the former rails were of Elizabethan character. A good view of the south aisle is obtained from here, particularly of the carvings on the roof. The room is reached by a circular staircase of stone. It has been supposed that the porch and room above were built at some time previous to the nave piers, but I cannot see why. Though good Early English, we see that it is not early in that period by the "plate tracery" window of the parvise, and by the flat under edges to the lowest members of the bases of the pillars.

Fig. 2.

The outer door (see Fig. 2) has a lovely trefoil top under a containing arch, and is very beautifully moulded.

THE EXTERIOR

can be seen from every side, owing to the isolated position of the church (see Plate IV.).

The west front presents several interesting features. The doorway, with an ordinary two-centred arch, has similar mouldings to the trefoil-headed door of the porch. The window above (now restored) is a slightly later form than that of the parvise, but the west end of the nave was often the last part to be finished, and both windows are evidently of the same *period*, though the parvise may be a few *years* earlier. The buttresses at the corners are massive, and not placed diagonally. All these features are Early English, but there are indications of earlier work in the buttresses on either side of the door and the string-course above. It is true that these buttresses project farther than the Norman ones on the south transept; but they are too broad for Early English work, and, when we bear in mind that the nave was probably finished after the transepts, and that all the Norman work in this church is late, we need not be surprised if buttresses built at this period partake of both Norman and Early English characteristics. The string-course, too, of the semi-hexagonal form, occurred more commonly in the Norman period than any other; so I think we have very fair evidence that the west

PLATE IV.

SHIFFNAL.

wall is Norman, and that therefore the Norman nave and aisles extended as far west as the present church does (see Plan). The cross on the gable is modern, as are the others, with the exception of that on the east of the Moreton chapel.

The rebuilt buttresses of the north aisle are similar to those at the west. The present entrance to the tower is modern, the old one being in the north wall of the north transept. The buttresses at this part are of rather a nondescript character, and were probably built after the fire. The windows, however, are I think earlier. They are poor, coarse specimens, but, if they had been Elizabethan, there would probably have been no cusps. Another argument is that there are several windows at Claverley, of pre-Reformation date, very like these. They are late Perpendicular, but not so late as 1592.

On the north side of the chancel there are some indications of the masonry having been disturbed, but is is difficult to see how the existing doorway in the north chancel wall can have opened into the supposed vestry. The Norman windows are much more ornate than on the inside (see Plate IV.). The hood-mouldings are similar, but here there are shafts: the abaci are round, shewing the late period of the style, and all the capitals are differently and curiously carved; the bases project in a peculiar manner. The buttress beyond the windows has suffered a good deal: about here the Norman chancel ended.

The east front is very fine, with its large remarkable window, and the beautiful quatrefoil above. The buttresses are not placed diagonally, as was commonly the case in the Decorated period, but, as we should expect, the projection at the top is about equal to the breadth.

In the south wall of the chancel is a very ornamental recess, of Decorated work: it has an open cinquefoiled arch, surmounted by an ogee canopy with pinnacles, crockets, and finial. We have no idea now what this recess was for: the recumbent effigy evidently does not belong to it. At this point the peculiarity of the masonry and string-course on the chapel wall, which I have already referred to, can be seen.

The early Decorated string-course and the later one on the chapel look exactly alike, but there is this characteristic difference, that the later one has a small roll or bowtell below the under-hollow of the course: the small bowtell in this position is very rare before the Perpendicular period. With the exceptions I have named, the walls of the Moreton chapel are entirely late Decorated,—a most remarkable thing, when it is remembered that there are Early English sedilia inside. The very late character of the Decorated work is shewn by the tracery of the west window of the chapel, almost Perpendicular, and by the hollowed hood-moulding. The niche above is not in the centre of the gable: is it possible that this is part of the Early English work? The buttresses of the chapel project farther than those of the chancel:

this is natural, as they are almost Perpendicular.   The basement moulding
shews the same period.   The doorway is well moulded, having the string-course,
just referred to, continued as the dripstone.

The most remarkable feature in the exterior of the south transept
is the remains of a very fine Norman doorway (see Fig. 3). It was three

Fig. 3.

times recessed, and the capitals still retain a good deal of their elaborate
carving.   The abaci here are square, but a late period in the style is, as
before, indicated by the bands.   Norman buttresses and string-courses also
remain on this wall.   The buttress in the middle of the old doorway (see Plan) is
probably Elizabethan, but the windows, though slightly different from those
on the north side, are probably earlier.   The parapet above has been recently
renewed and raised to suit the internal juncture with the south tower arch.
The windows of the south aisle have already been mentioned: the buttresses
are probably Elizabethan.

The exterior view of the porch and parvise above is quaint and
remarkable.   The tower, though very plain, has a dignified appearance.   It is
massive and square, with a stair-turret at the north west corner.   The
battlement has been renewed.   The windows are plain lancets: some have
thought that they originally had tracery ; the date I have assigned (circa 1250)
would fit in quite well with an early form of tracery.   The upper story is

slightly narrower than the lower part. The pitch of the old roofs can be seen, particularly on the north and south sides.

A peculiar inscription appears on the churchyard wall, west of the entrance gate :—

OPE SOLA GULIELMI WALFORD, VIRI PLURIMUM AMICI TANDEM
RESURGO. 1691.

The parish register goes back to 1678. The communion plate is modern ; but an ancient chalice, which formerly belonged to the parish, was discovered a few years ago in Yorkshire, and presented to the Roman Catholic chapel at Shiffnal by Lord Stafford. It has the inscription :—

RESTORE MEE TO SHEAFNAL IN SHROPSHIRE.

Stockton.

St. Chad.

IN the *Antiquities of Shropshire*, the Rev. R. W. Eyton observes that he has no proof of a church here before the 13th century, but he shews inferentially that the church was probably founded, either partly or entirely, by De Laci, Lord of Higford in the parish, very shortly after Domesday.

The architectural evidence fits in with this theory, for the Norman work may quite possibly belong to the end of the 11th century.

The church underwent very considerable "restoration" between 1858 and 1860, at the hands of the late Mr. T. C. Whitmore, the squire of the parish, who took the greatest interest in the work, and laboured with his own hands at it. The result cannot be said to be very satisfactory, and one sadly regrets the destruction of the old work. Still, the renovation was done thoroughly well from a structural point of view, and the church is in a very substantial condition.

In one respect Mr. Whitmore left an example many "restorers" would do well to copy,—in handing down a careful record of the state of the church at the time, and the alterations that were made.

From this account, and from old photographs, I have been able to gather the following information about the church in 1857.

The earliest work in the church was Norman, possibly of the period already referred to. The nave and chancel were built at this time, and the photographs shew Norman windows on the north and south sides of the chancel, and a semi-circular-headed doorway on the south: the former buttresses on the south of the nave also had a Norman appearance. Additions seem to have been made in the Decorated period, one traceried window in that style being shewn on the south side of the chancel. The tower would appear to have been built in the 15th century, but the upper part rebuilt in the 17th; and at this late period battlements were placed along the nave walls, and windows inserted in the nave and the east wall of the chancel. A debased porch existed on the west side of the tower.

To come to the church as it now stands, we notice a great change, and should be inclined at first to put the whole of it down as modern, with the exception of the tower. However, the inner part of the walls is probably old, as we are told that they were refaced internally and externally. In the chancel we notice a kind of "mock" piscina, aumbry, and sedilia on the south side, and a recess on the north. The old ones existed in 1857, and were built round in this way: part of the old basin of the piscina and some ancient tiles are on the window-sill near. The Norman window opposite was retained, and another, preserved elsewhere, was displaced when the organ was built. There is a narrow square-headed window on the south, described as a leper window: it is probably of the 14th century. The communion table is Elizabethan. In the vestry is an old chest, with good ironwork, bearing the date 1696. The roof of the chancel was retained, and is late Perpendicular, with carved panelling and battlement.

The chancel arch and all the windows of the chancel and nave not already mentioned are modern. The nave has very small transepts on either side: these existed before the restoration. Some beautiful Jacobean carving, with designs of fruit and flowers, was worked into the pulpit and reading-desk, and the pews, altered to their present form, are probably of the same date. The waggon roof of the nave is peculiar: the boarding may be of this period; the carved brackets are modern. The font is one of the best things in the church, and is Perpendicular. It is panelled, and has a variety of leaves represented in conventional form: the quatrefoils are filled with flowers.

The tower arch has poor mouldings: the pillars are cut into wide hollow chamfers, in a manner probably distinctive of late Perpendicular work. The tower was evidently built at two different periods, as the character of the masonry outside shews. The later part is about one-third of the whole, and is built of a poorer stone than the earlier: the upper part has debased Perpendicular windows, and may well have been built in the 17th century. It is interesting to note that this late work was probably a rebuilding, and not an addition to the church, for it will be observed that the old stone in the buttresses goes up to the same height as the old stone in the walls. Now buttresses do not generally go up to the very top of a tower, and so it is probable that the old tower here was considerably loftier than the present altitude of the old stone. The west window is modern, and the debased porch has been swept away.

Three of the bells date back to the 17th century. The tenor bell has a beautiful inscription which supplies important historical evidence with regard to the church. It is:—

GLORIA IN EXCELSIS DEO PATRI. FILIO. ET SPIRITUI SANCTO. JOHN LEE THO. EARMER WAR: GULIELMUS WHITMORE MILES HUJUS ECCLESIÆ PATRONUS ET INSTAURATOR. IPSE IN ECCLESIAM TRIUMPHANTEM ADSCITUS, ME ECCLESIÆ MILITANTIS USUM VOVIT ET DESIGNAVIT. 1651.

This shews that Sir William Whitmore was already dead in 1651, and had been the "restorer" of the church,—prior to the Civil War we may suppose. We now have an explanation of the large amount of work done to the church in the early part of the 17th century. To that time we may probably assign the upper part of the tower, the carved work on the pulpit and reading-desk, the nave roof and pews, besides the late windows and battlements removed 35 years ago.

The church possesses an old chalice, of post-Reformation date: it has a top, which may have been used as a paten. The register dates back to 1558.

Sutton Maddock.

St. Mary.

THERE was a church here prior to 1186-7, when the advowson was given to Wombridge Priory, but in Saxon times Sutton was included in the large parish of Shiffnal. The present building has little architectural interest. The body of the church till recently was of Georgian character: it was rebuilt in modern Gothic style in 1887, and consists of nave, chancel, south porch, and vestry on the north side.

The only ancient part is the tower, which is late Perpendicular. There is a peculiar device over the east window with the date 1579. This may well be the date of the whole tower, which is not of any great beauty. The internal arch has broad, coarse, mouldings, and the upper square-headed windows have no cusps. The west window has three lights and is pointed, but there is no tracery: over the south window is some rude carving. There are diagonal buttresses; and the tower is finished with a battlement and pinnacles.

There is an Elizabethan table in the vestry. The parish register dates from 1559. There is a post-Reformation chalice, with the top used as a paten.

Tong.

St. Bartholomew.

THIS most interesting building is one of the few parish churches that we can definitely refer to a particular period by means of MS. record. We find that Elizabeth, widow of Sir Fulke de Pembruge, purchased the advowson of the church from Shrewsbury Abbey in 1410, and converted it into a Collegiate Church. The greater portion of the building is therefore of this period, but there are clear indications of earlier work.

The first mention we have of the church is in the 11th century, when it was endowed and given to Shrewsbury Abbey by Earl Roger de Montgomery, before 1094. No remains of this building exist, and there is no record of any addition to the church till the 15th century. The architecture however, as usual, supplies us with evidence; for, part of the southern arcade of the nave is Early English in character, probably of the middle of the 13th century. It will be presently shewn that the nave of the church was probably where the south aisle now is. So far as we can tell, this nave may have been the original early Norman one, and the Early English north aisle may have been an addition to it. However that may be, the present southern arcade shews us clearly that there was a church here with nave and one aisle in the 13th century.

Most of the building, as before remarked, is of the early part of the 15th century, and is of very good, if somewhat plain, early Perpendicular character. At this time, the church was built to consist of chancel, with vestry on the north side; central tower, and small spire; nave and aisles, and south porch, the early arcade being retained to separate the nave from the south aisle.

The fine stalls and screens were probably erected some years later; and the Vernon chapel, south of the tower and south aisle, was built by Sir Henry Vernon in 1515.

The old work in the church is in a wonderful state of preservation, and the magnificent tombs have, to a great extent, escaped the mutilation which has so commonly befallen the monuments of our forefathers.

A very careful restoration of the church has lately (1892) taken place, Mr. Ewan Christian being the architect, and Mr. Bowdler, of Shrewsbury, the builder.

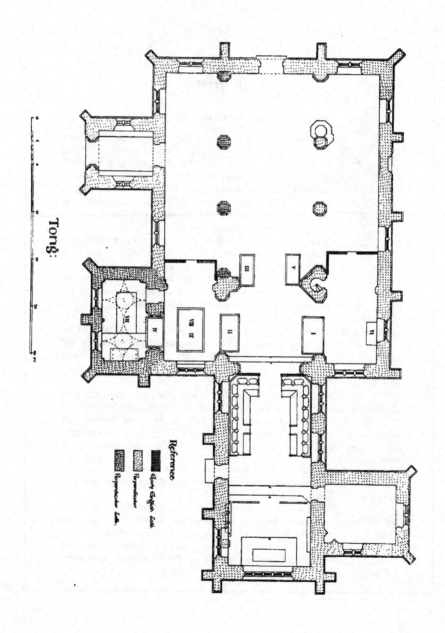

Tong:

Reference
Early English Work
Perpendicular
Reproduction Late

A great deal of information with regard to the church and the families which have possessed Tong Castle, will be found in Mr. G. Griffiths' excellent *Guide to Tong Church*. I will, as usual, chiefly confine myself to a description of the architectural features.

THE CHANCEL

is early Perpendicular, like the greater portion of the church. Here and there the details partake of the Decorated character, which is not surprising, considering the date. In the east window, for example, though the tracery is clearly Perpendicular, the outer moulding, going round the arch is a double ogee of Decorated form, the convex part being greater than the concave. The window, which is rather nearer the south wall than the north, has some fragments of 15th century glass, which have lately been carefully re-arranged. Of the three south windows, the middle one has similar mouldings to the east window, but those of the other two and of the two windows on the north side are plainer. The piscina shews the same character: it has two small pillars inside, no doubt for supporting a shelf, and is, as usual, in the south wall. There are three sedilia, arched over, with cusps in the form of plain Tudor flowers. Against the east wall are two small brass tablets, dated 1549 and 1550: the Elizabethan details are of no special interest. Above these are the remains of two canopies, which have been cut away to allow of the Ten Commandments being placed there. In the south wall is a monument to Mrs. Wylde, daughter of Sir Thomas Harries of Tong. The details are Classical, with no admixture of Gothic, and the date is 1624. A female figure, in the costume of the period, is represented in a kneeling posture. The other monuments in this part of the church are of no great interest. They are to Lord Pierrepoint, d. 1715; Lord Middleton, d. 1734; and to the Durants, who owned the Castle from 1760 to 1855.

The old Priest's door remains in the south wall, the woodwork being apparently original, under a four-centred arch.

The most remarkable and beautiful feature of the chancel is the highly-carved choir stalls and screen (see Plate V.). Behind these are a number of consecration crosses, shewing that the stalls were not here in 1410: they are, however, of very good Perpendicular design, and may have been added at almost any time in the 15th century. There are six stalls on each side, and four next the screen, looking east. The stalls were numbered in 1806: they all have misereres of good workmanship. The panelling behind the fourth stall is more elaborate than the rest: it is supposed that this was assigned to the Warden of the College. All the panelling is very good, with quatre-foils, Tudor flowers and roses. Some of the standards are beautifully carved: the cornice has representations of birds, grapes, etc. The whole is wonderfully preserved, considering its age, but parts of the work, especially the upper part of the cornice, have lately been renewed with very good carving.

The roof of the chancel is original: it is nearly flat, and is supported on stone corbels, which are mostly old and well carved. The communion table is modern, but the chair near is Elizabethan.

THE VESTRY

is of the same period as the greater portion of the church, but the windows are plainer and the roof is of a low pitch. The doorway has a good four-centred arch, the spandrels being filled with tracery: the original door remains, with some good carving, and three peculiar holes, the use of which it is difficult to explain. The Decorated form again appears in the wave moulding round the doorway, which has a broad convex part: a later Perpendicular example would have had broader concave parts.

The most striking object in the vestry is the mediæval embroidery in a case against the south wall: it is an elaborate piece of work in various colours, and ornamented with cherubs, flowers, and other designs. The nuns of the neighbouring convent of White Ladies are supposed to have worked it: if so, it must be at least 350 years old. The library of 410 volumes was presented by Lord Pierrepoint some 200 years ago. There is an old chest and table, and an Elizabethan chair with the cross-bars missing.

Going westwards our attention is at once directed to

THE TOMBS,

which must be described under a separate heading. Very few parish churches can boast of such a wonderful collection, illustrating architectural ornament, and armour and costume, from the beginning of the 15th to the beginning of the 17th century.

The important tombs are numbered on the Ground Plan in chronological order, and will be so described.

No. I. (see Plates VII. and VI.) is in all probability the tomb of Sir Fulke de Pembruge and Dame Elizabeth, his wife. Mr. Eyton, in his *Antiquities of Shropshire*, assigns it to Sir Richard Vernon and wife, but, as it seems to me, Mr. Griffiths, in his *Guide to Tong Church*, effectually disproves this theory. For this, as will presently be shewn, the character of the armour is sufficient evidence; Sir Richard Vernon did not die till 1451 or 1452, and the style of armour here seen went out of fashion some 40 years before that date.

Sir Fulke de Pembruge was lord of Tong in 1371, and died in 1408 or 1409: his crest was a Turkish woman's head, which is represented under the head of the figure. Dame Elizabeth, as before mentioned, was the

PLATE V

TONG.
LOOKING WEST.

foundress of the Collegiate Church: she died in 1446 or 1447, and is represented beside her husband, her head resting upon a pillow with angel supporters.

The architectural ornament of the tomb is of early Perpendicular character, with panelling, plain shields, and large square flowers. There is a break in the carving on the east side, and it has been supposed that the ornament originally belonged to one or more tombs, now destroyed.

No. II. (see Plates VI. and VII.) commemorates Sir Richard Vernon and his wife, Benedicta, daughter of Sir John Ludlow. He was Speaker of the Parliament held at Leicester in 1426, and was nephew and successor of Sir Fulke de Pembruge. The knight's head is supported by the family crest, a boar's head, and his wife's by a cushion and angels. He died in 1451.

There is some very elaborate canopy work at the sides of the tomb, with crockets and pinnacles of good Perpendicular character. The figures are of saints and angels alternately, the latter bearing plain shields. The whole of this alabaster tomb is of beautiful design, and the carving of figures and ornaments of exquisite workmanship.

No. III. is the monument of Sir William Vernon and his wife, Margaret, daughter and heiress of Sir William Twynfen, knight.

The lower part has some good Perpendicular work, with multi-foils enclosing shields and four-leaf flowers, but the chief interest lies in the upper part, which is a very good brass, inlaid in Purbeck marble. An inscription on the surrounding bevel records that Sir William was the son and heir of Sir Richard Vernon, and died in 1467 (see Plate X.). Figures of the sons and daughters are represented below those of the knight and his wife. There are several coats of arms. The ornamental part of the tomb ceases on the south side: this may have originally joined up to a stone pulpit.

No. IV. (see Plate VIII.) is that of Sir Henry Vernon and his wife, Lady Anne. Sir Henry was the founder of the Vernon Chapel: he was son of Sir William Vernon, and guardian and treasurer to Arthur, Prince of Wales, the elder brother of Henry VIII. His wife was a Talbot, daughter of the second Earl of Shrewsbury: she died in 1494 and her husband 21 years later.

This tomb is under an elliptical, or Burgundian, arch, between the south aisle and the Vernon Chapel. The architectural ornament is late Perpendicular with depressed arches, crocketed canopies, and imitation vaulting, figures, and shields. The colouring is blue and gold, and the whole work very elaborate. The general effect, however, especially of the figures, is not nearly so pleasing as that of the earlier tombs. There are some very rich canopies on the wall above, from which the images have gone (see Plate VII.).

Very similar carving adorns No. V. (see Plates V. and X.), which is the tomb of Richard Vernon, Esquire, and his wife, Margaret. The lower part, till quite recently, formed the communion table, being probably adapted as such

in the 18th century : it is now restored to its original position.   Richard
Vernon was the eldest son of Sir Henry, and died comparatively young in 1517.
His wife was daughter of Sir Robert Dymoke, the King's Champion.

No. VI. probably commemorates Humphrey, third son of Sir
Henry Vernon, and his wife, Alice, daughter and co-heiress of Sir John Ludlow
of Hodnet.   He died in 1542 or 1545, and his wife in 1531.   The figures
are incised on a slab, very much worn : part of the inscription remains on
the east side.

No. VII. is described elsewhere.

Nos. VIII. and IX. form a very elaborate Elizabethan monument
(see Plates VIII. and VII.).   There are four ugly obelisks at the corners, but
the work below is very rich, with Doric columns supporting round arches and
ornaments of Renaissance character.   The upper figures are those of the Hon.
Sir Thomas Stanley, second son of the third Earl of Derby, and his wife,
Margaret.   The latter was co-heiress of Sir George Vernon with the celebrated
Dorothy Vernon, who eloped with Sir John Manners on the night of her
sister's wedding, conveying Haddon Hall to the Rutland family.   Sir Thomas
Stanley died in 1576, and was succeeded by his son, Sir Edward, who is
represented below : he died in 1632.

This tomb formerly stood in the chancel, but was removed to
make way for the Durant monument towards the end of the last century.
Till recently it stood north and south.   The lines at the head of the tomb
have been ascribed to Shakespeare, and are therefore quoted here :

"Not monumentall stone preserves our fame
Nor sky aspyring piramids our name
The memory of him for whom this stands
Shall outlyve marbl and defacers' hands
When all to tyme's consumption shall be geaven
Standly for whom this stands shall stand in heaven."

The lines at the other end are very poor in comparison.

Any account of these wonderful tombs would be very incomplete,
which did not call attention to the different styles of armour exemplified
thereon.   Mediæval armour has been divided into the following periods[*] :—

(1.)   The Surcoat Period, ending circa 1307.

(2.)   The Cyclas Period, circa 1325—1350.

(3.)   The Camail Period, circa 1350—1410.

(4.)   The Lancastrian Period, circa 1410—1455.

(5.)   The Yorkist Period, circa 1455—1485.

(6.)   The Early Tudor Period, circa 1485—1558.

(7.)   The Elizabethan Period, circa 1558—1680.

[*] See Rev. H. W. Macklin's excellent manual on " Monumental Brasses," published by
Swan Sonnenschein & Co.

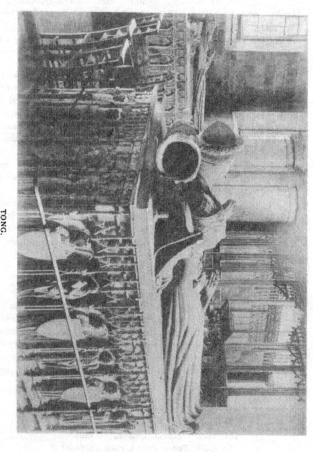

TONG.
LOOKING NORTH.

PLATE. VII.

TONG.

LOOKING SOUTH.

We have at Tong examples of no less than five of these,—one of the Camail, one of the Lancastrian, one of the Yorkist, three of the Early Tudor, and two of the Elizabethan Period. Such a collection is, I should think, unique in a parish church.

First the Camail; on No. I., the tomb of Sir Fulke de Pembruge, circa 1410. We have here the following characteristic marks of the style (see Plate VII.).

(1.) The bascinet, an acutely pointed cap.

(2.) The camail, the tippet of mail covering the neck and shoulders.

(3.) The mail shirt, visible here at the armpits, elbows, and at the bottom.

(4.) The jupon, a tight fitting tunic without sleeves, fringed at the bottom.

(5.) The bawdric, or ornamental belt: the sword and misericorde (short dagger) have been cut away, but remains of the attachments to the bawdric can be seen on the left and right respectively.

(6.) On the arms we see the épaulières protecting the shoulders; the coutes at the elbows, brassarts above and vambraces below; gauntlets on the hands.

(7.) On the legs there are cuisses, protecting the thighs; genouillières on the knees, jambs on the legs; on the feet, sharp-toed "sollerets," and a gusset of mail protecting the insteps. The spurs have been cut away, but were evidently of the rowell or wheel type. The feet rest against a lion.

Next we come to No. II., the tomb of Sir Richard Vernon, circa 1452, which will illustrate the alterations in armour which took place in the Lancastrian period (see Plate VI.).

(1.) The acute bascinet gives way to a lower helmet.

(2.) The camail is replaced by a steel gorget.

(3.) The jupon being abandoned, we can see the armour, consisting of a cuirass on the breast, and below this—

(4.) A skirt of "taces," or broad hoops of steel, fastened to one another; below are buckled "tuilles," a sign that this tomb is *late* in the Lancastrian period.

(5.) The bawdric is still shewn, though it has usually disappeared before this period. But there is also another belt, tied loosely across, supporting the sword on the left and the dagger on the right: what is left of the sword is of beautiful workmanship and has the letters IHS carved on it. There is a collar round the necks of the knight and his lady, with the letters SS, a mark of honour introduced by Henry IV.

(6.) On the arms are three épaulières, at the shoulders and below "pauldrons," another late sign. The coutes are like shells and almost fan-shaped. There are gauntlets as before.

(7.) On the legs is no thigh armour, but the genouillières have two plates above and below: below are armour plates, and, as before, we have pointed sollerets and rowell spurs, but no gusset of mail. The feet rest against a lion.

This is well called the Complete Plate Period; no mail whatever appears on this example.

The next period, the Yorkist, is represented by No. III., the brass of Sir William Vernon, circa 1467. In the few years which transpired between 1452 and 1467, great changes in armour took place and we here see the extraordinary fashion that was prevalent during the Wars of the Roses.

(1.) The helmet is not represented; the hair is short as was generally the case early in this style.

(2.) The gorget gives way to the collar of mail, very different, however, from the camail.

(3.) The cuirass is covered with "placcates" and "demi-placcates."

(4.) The skirt of taces is reduced in size and the tuilles increased: between these is a baguette of mail.

(5.) The bawdric has disappeared, and a loose belt supports the sword: the dagger is attached to the skirt.

(6.) On the arms we see pauldrons, coutes, and gauntlets, of enormous size.

(7.) The legs are covered with armour: the sollerets are still pointed, and the spurs are of the rowell form.

Altogether this brass shews us very clearly the massive and ungainly character of the armour of the time.

The Early Tudor period is shewn on the effigies of Sir Henry Vernon, Richard Vernon, and Humphrey Vernon. I will describe that on the first-named, No. IV. (see Plate VIII.).

(1.) As in the Yorkist period, the helmet is not shewn, but the hair is longer than at that time.

(2.) The collar of mail is retained.

(3.) The awkward placcates and demi-placcates disappear, and the cuirass is clearly shewn.

(4.) The taces are smaller, and the tuilles, four in number, larger; and underneath appears the mail skirt, the distinguishing feature of the period.

(5.) The loose belt is retained, supporting the sword and dagger: the SS collar is worn.

PLATE. VIII.

TONG.

FROM THE VERNON CHAPEL.

(6.) Epaulières re-appear on the shoulders, but pauldrons are also used, with the inner parts turned up : these are called pass-guards. The coutes are larger than we often have them at this period. The gauntlets are not on the hands, but are often seen, as on the tomb of Richard Vernon, lying by the side of the figure.

(7.) The genouillières have plates above and below : the great change in the lower armour is the substitution of round sabbatons for pointed sollerets.

The armour of the last, or Elizabethan, period is shewn on the tombs of Sir Thomas Stanley and Sir Edward Stanley, Nos. VIII. and IX. (see Plates VIII. and VII.).

(1.) The hair is depicted as before.

(2.) The collar is no longer of mail or steel, but we have the ruff on the upper figure, and the wide Stuart collar, which succeeded it, on the lower.

(3.) The cuirass is sharply ridged down the breast.

(4.) Taces disappear, and the skirt is composed of tassets or lamboys, a development of the tuilles, buckled to the cuirass.

(5.) The belt becomes smaller and is placed directly across the body.

(6.) Pauldrons are now finally discarded : the épaulières are ornamental and almost meet across the breast : coutes are still worn, but not gauntlets.

(7.) The legs are fully protected, there being several plates above the genouillières : the feet have been cut away, but the shoes were broad ; the rowell spurs shew well, especially on the upper figure.

Periods are not so distinctly marked in ladies' costume as in armour ; some of the head-dresses, however, may be noticed with advantage. That of the wife of Sir Richard Vernon is a beautifully carved example of the horned head-dress which prevailed at the time of Henry V. and onwards (see Plate VI.). The extraordinary butterfly head-dress of the Yorkist period is shewn on the small female figures on the brass. A plain pedimental head-dress appears on the tomb opposite, and finally the Mary Queen of Scots cap on the Elizabethan tomb (see Plate VIII.). Dame Elizabeth de Pembruge on the earliest monument, and Dame Margaret Vernon on the brass, have the costume of widows, with a wimple round the neck.

THE VERNON CHAPEL

was built by Sir Henry Vernon in 1515, and is quite a gem of the late Perpendicular style. The most striking architectural feature is, of course, the roof, which is a beautiful example of fan vaulting (see Plate IX.). It is supported by two half conoids in the centre and four quarter conoids at the corners: in the spaces left by the conoids two graceful and highly ornamented pendants hang down. The eastern one is carved with leaves, the other is larger and has the Vernon arms. The northern conoid ends with another pendant, which has carvings of grapes and vine leaves, of bolder appearance than one often sees in Perpendicular work. The whole design of the roof is very graceful, and about as good an example of a small conoidal roof as one can see anywhere. Remains of the gilding can be seen, especially on the western pendant and the canopy: from this feature the chapel has often been called the Golden Chapel.

The figure on the west wall (see Plate IX.) is in the attitude of preaching, the left hand uplifted, and the right hand turning the leaves of a book: the canopy above is very rich, and has four angels bearing the arms of the Vernons and allied families. The architectural character is, of course, Perpendicular, with Tudor flowers as a crest, flat foliage, imitation vaulting, and strictly Perpendicular crockets. This figure is no doubt that of (Sir) Arthur Vernon, rector of Whitchurch, and youngest son of Sir Henry Vernon. His brass (No. VII.) has lately been rediscovered on the floor, in a very perfect state. It was described by Cole, the celebrated antiquary, in 1757, but it must have been covered up some time afterwards. The figure, in clerical attire, is about 3 ft. 6 in. long: we learn from the inscription that he was an M.A. of Cambridge. There are four coats of arms at the corners, and over the figure a representation of a chalice and paten. There are a number of ancient tiles on the floor of the chapel.

The east wall has an inscription recording a request to "PRAY FOR THE SOWLE OF SYR HARIE VERNON KNYGHT AND DAME ANNE HYS WYFE," also "FOR THE SOLL OF SIR ARTHUR VERNON PRYST." Over this is the remains of a representation of the Crucifixion.

The old altar slab till recently formed part of the pavement: it has now been refixed, probably in the original position. It has the usual five crosses, one at each corner and a larger one in the middle. Besides these, however, there are two small rude crosses incised on the stone. It is difficult to say what these were for: a large number of consecration crosses appear in the church, and I can only hazard the suggestion that these two were for that purpose, but it was certainly not the custom to place them on the altar slab.

The east wall contains an opening that one would imagine to be an aumbry, but there is no sign of a place for a shutter. The recess contained, when recently opened, what was apparently the mouldy remains of a loaf of bread.

The south wall has a small piscina with a depressed arch, but no signs of a drain. The windows are double lights, the arches being of the four-centred form. As is common at this late period, there are no cusps. There are three consecration crosses on the south wall, and at least one on the north.

TONG.

GROINED ROOF IN THE VERNON CHAPEL.

The mouldings are of the usual Perpendicular character: the abaci of the pillars begin with straight slopes and have ogees underneath; the bases are bell-shaped. There is a very characteristic example of a Perpendicular wave-moulding on the north wall (see Plate IX.), the concave parts being wide and the convex part acutely projecting.

Nearly all the wood-work is modern, but one of the old standards remains, and part of the panelling.

The entrance to the chapel has an ogee arch: the mouldings are very poor; the abaci and bases are of the usual form, as just described, and the plinths very much raised from the ground; the crockets are different from those on the canopy inside, but still Perpendicular, of rather square form.

THE NAVE AND AISLES.

At first sight the north and south arcades of the nave appear to be the same, but several differences will soon be noticed. The north arcade is more lofty than the south, and the mouldings are different: the arches on the north have wave-mouldings similar to those in the chancel, already described as being more of the Decorated than the Perpendicular form; the arches on the south have plain chamfers, but the mouldings of the capitals and bases are quite sufficient to shew that the south arcade is earlier than the north.

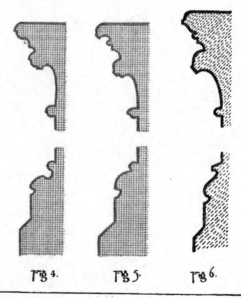

Fig 4.   Fig 5.   Fig 6.

Take first the west respond on the south side (see Fig. 4).
The abacus has the scroll moulding, which only occurs in the Decorated
period and the latter part of the Early English : the moulding below is an
ornamental one, of small pyramids ; this does not occur after the Early
English period. The base has the hollow moulding, which will hold water,
a sure sign, of course, of Early English work. The next pillar is very
interesting (see Fig. 5). The abacus is undercut in the Early English manner,
but the base has the flat under edge, an indication, as has been before
remarked (in the description of Shiffnal Church), of Decorated or late
Early English work. We see that the mouldings combine Early
English and Decorated characteristics, the former predominating, and we
cannot then be far wrong in referring the arcade to the transition between
these two periods, say circa 1260. The bases of the other two columns are
like that in Fig. 5, but it is remarkable that the capitals resemble the early
Perpendicular ones on the north arcade and the tower (see Plate X.
and Fig. 6). These must have been altered from the Early English form,
probably on account of decay, in 1410. To make this theory of the date of
the arcade doubly sure, we have a hood-moulding on the south side, of Early
English form. The undercutting is shallower than usual, but the corbels are
either mask ornaments or of stiff-leaf foliage, in both cases of Early English
design.

A hood-moulding inside a building is of course a pure ornament,
and, when there was only one over an arcade, it was generally towards the
nave and not towards the aisle. It seems probable then that the present
south aisle took the place of the nave, the original north aisle occupying
part of the space of the present nave. Whether the old nave was Early
English, or part of the original church founded by Roger de Montgomery ;
and how wide nave and aisle were, we cannot now determine.

The mouldings of the early Perpendicular columns are interesting
(see Plates VI. and X., and Fig. 6). The abacus is losing the scroll form
of the Decorated, and assuming the usual type of the succeeding style, but
the upper edge is still a curve and not a slope. The base is becoming bell-
shaped, the under edge being round instead of flat, which it would have
been in the Decorated period.* There is a hood-moulding over the chancel
arch, but not over the other tower arches.

The roofs of nave and aisles are nearly flat but are very good,
especially that of the nave, which has fine carvings of angels with shields,
square flowers and leaves, and the original ornamental stone corbels.

Some of the tracery in the west window has been renewed :
there are some fragments of ancient glass ; one has a representation of a

---

* On the Plan, the hatching of most of the building should be referred to as " Perpendicular Early,"
instead of " Perpendicular."

TONG.

LOOKING EAST.

jewelled mitre. The other windows are of plain Perpendicular design.

East of tomb No. VI., is an ancient incised slab, which was discovered at the recent restoration. The lines are so much worn that it is difficult to decipher what they represent : from the character of the few letters that remain I think it must be at least as early as the 13th century. There are some remains of another tomb, fixed to the north wall, where there was formerly a door. These are not unlike the carving on the east side of No. I., and it is supposed that the length of the fingers, and other characteristics, point to an early date, but the architectural design is Perpendicular, with angels, square crockets, and battlements.

The belfry is entered by a stone staircase from the north aisle. There are eight bells, one of which is celebrated for its great size : it was given by Sir Henry Vernon, but the date, 1518, shews it to have been made after his death.

The screen in the north aisle is not so fine as that in the south : Perpendicular tracery is more fully carried out, the arches are more depressed, and there are square flowers instead of wreaths (see Plate X.). That in the south aisle (see Plate VIII.) is very similar to the chancel screen, and therefore very beautiful. There is a small late brass on the wall near. A good deal of Perpendicular carved work remains on the pews. The pulpit is Jacobean, of date 1629 (see Plate X.). Above is the old entrance to the rood-loft from the belfry staircase, now almost blocked.

The font is against the north-west pillar : it is octagonal and of Perpendicular design, with shields and ornamental cusps. Besides the usual steps, there is one on the north side, of peculiar shape, for the sponsor (see Plan).

THE PORCH,

like the rest of the church, is in a very good state of preservation. There are stone seats on either side, and the original roof remains. There are two Perpendicular windows, and the wave-moulding already noticed occurs on the outer and inner doorways : over the latter is a niche, but the figure has disappeared.

THE EXTERIOR.

The most striking feature outside the church is undoubtedly the graceful tower and spire (see Plate XI.). A central tower is of course very rare in the Perpendicular period, and the particular form of this must, I think, be almost unique in England. The lower part is square, and this supports an octagon, which has a small spire rising from within a battlement : this is of the Perpendicular form, with horizontal and vertical moulding and pinnacles. A battlement of this character goes all round the church, and there is no steep gable : the present pitch of the roofs is original.

The details on the Vernon chapel are different in several respects from those on the chancel and the rest of the building, and it is interesting to compare the early and late Perpendicular forms. The chapel windows are much more depressed than the others, and have no cusps. The pinnacles, though more elaborate, are not nearly so graceful as the earlier ones. The basement moulding is more decidedly of the bell-shape in the late than in the early work: the window mouldings, too, differ.

The east window of the south aisle is different from the chancel windows, but was, of course, not part of the old church, as it is Perpendicular.

The hood-mouldings of the tower windows are hollowed out in the usual Perpendicular fashion, but those of the chancel are not so pronounced, and a string-course occurs there and on the porch, with a heavy ogee where the hollow often occurs.

The buttresses at the corners of the porch and chapel are diagonal, but, at the east end, buttresses are placed at right angles to one another. Those at the north-east corner have niches with crockets and imitation vaulting: the supporting corbels are carved with leaves curling over in the Perpendicular form; there are no figures now. There are a number of grotesque gargoyles on the church. The vestry, though of the same period as most of the church, is of poorer design, the windows not being nearly so good. On the north wall, especially near the blocked Perpendicular door, there are marks of Cromwell's cannon balls. It is supposed that his friendship for the Hon. William Pierrepoint, the owner of Tong at the time, preserved the church and monuments from further destruction.

The west front is plain but effective. Some distance west of the church, and considerably below its level, are the remains of some almshouses. There is said to have been a chapel connected with them, but it is impossible to say exactly where it was. The architectural detail shews the work to be of the 15th century. The college stood some distance to the south of the church: the marks of the foundations can sometimes be distinguished.

The cross in the churchyard has been converted into a sun-dial, as is so commonly the case: it bears the date 1776.

The communion plate is chiefly remarkable for the beautiful ciborium, probably of the early part of the 16th century. It seems to have been used to contain the reserved sacrament, and is now probably unique. It is of silver gilt, beautifully chased, and has a small compartment made of crystal.

The parish register dates back to 1620.

In conclusion it may be interesting to mention that it is very probable, if not certain, that Tong is the old church described by Charles Dickens in the latter part of *The Old Curiosity Shop*. The description, however, cannot be said to be very accurate.

PLATE XI.

TONG.

Worfield.

St. Peter or St. Matthew.

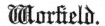

HERE was a church here at the time of Domesday, but there are now no remains of that early period. The appearance of parts of the present edifice is rather puzzling: the probable history of it is as follows:—

The oldest part of the building is of Early English date, when a church seems to have been erected with, at least, nave and south-west tower.

About the end of the 13th century, the building was considerably enlarged, a large chancel, and probably, north and south transepts being erected.

In the late Decorated period, another great alteration took place, in the building of north and south aisles, including the former transepts.

Shortly afterwards, in early Perpendicular times, the tower was rebuilt in about the same position, and the south aisle extended westwards to meet it, the lofty spire being added at the same time.

In the 18th century, new windows were inserted in the chancel, and a south porch erected. These features were swept away in 1861-2, when the church underwent an extensive restoration, at the hands of Messrs. F. and H. Francis. New windows were inserted in the chancel, and at the west end of the nave and tower: the tracery of some of the windows was renewed, galleries and plaster ceilings removed, and the Classical porch replaced by the present one. A good deal was also done to the roofs, and other alterations to the seating, floors, etc., carried out.

THE CHANCEL

now presents a very modern appearance, but the general effect is decidedly good. The windows must be a great improvement on the debased ones they replaced. The piscina and sedilia have been restored: one of the stones in the former seems to be original. The chair opposite is of late Perpendicular character. The roof is modern, of good design. There is a fine chancel screen, with ornamental cusps, quatrefoils, battlements, and Perpendicular tracery. The chancel arch was raised a few years ago, but the old work is retained, and is most curious. At first sight one would be inclined to say that the square abaci were of the end of the 12th century, but they are in reality much later, for, at the corners of the north capital, are distinct carvings of the ball-flower: on the south capital, heads are found in the same position. The ball-flower is, of course, a sign of Decorated work, and this, combined with the undercutting of the capitals, seems to indicate the end of the 13th century as the date of the arch. A wave moulding of Decorated character is also seen on the arch and jambs. There is a relieving arch above.

THE NAVE.

The peculiar appearance of the first bay on either side must first be noticed. Why is it that the arcading, separating nave from aisles, does not commence in the usual way against the east wall? The most probable explanation seems to me to be that there were transepts, but not aisles, in the early Decorated period, and that, when the aisles were built in late Decorated times, most of the *west* walls of the transepts were removed, leaving the inner extremities standing, from which the arcades were continued westwards. The late Decorated nave was *slightly* wider than before, and so the early Decorated arches to the transepts could not be retained. These were therefore removed, and the spaces between the east wall and the remaining portions of the west walls of the transepts arched over anew, with mouldings similar to those of the arcades. This explanation may seem to be a little far-fetched, but it is the only way I can account for the very unusual appearance. More of the early Decorated detail was left on the south side than on the north: there is a respond against the east wall, very similar to those of the chancel arch. The small column above this looks like a vaulting shaft, but its position is peculiar, and there is no sign of any vaulting having been carried out.

The roofs of the nave and aisles are partly original: the pulpit is modern. Some of the old Perpendicular woodwork remains on the seats.

In the south wall of the nave, west of the arcade, is some early work, presumably a piscina and an aumbry, but there are no remains of a drain, and the position is uncommon. However, it is fairly certain that the work is Early English. Over the piscina are two arches, but no tracery between them and the outer hood-moulding. There is no clerestory: the nave and aisles are almost of equal height.

THE NORTH AISLE

is separated from the nave by four arches, resting on octagonal columns, besides the eastern arch already referred to. The mouldings on the columns are interesting, clearly indicating the *late* Decorated period: the scroll is no longer seen on the abacus, which assumes the Perpendicular form; the base

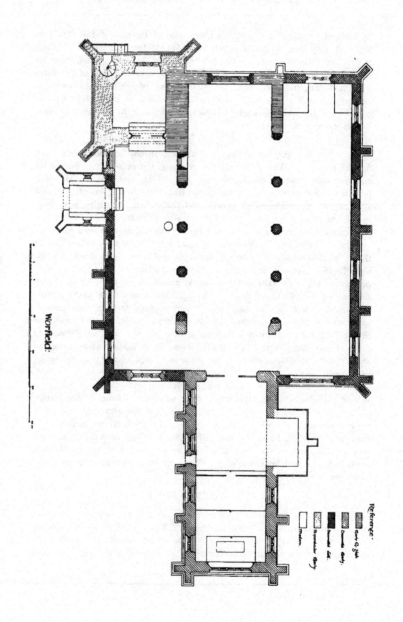

Worfield:

Reference:

is almost bell-shaped, but the Decorated character is maintained by the flat under edge, which can be noticed on the eastern respond. The hood-mouldings are hollowed, and terminate in heads. I will refer later to the windows. Some remarkable mouldings should be noticed on that part of the south wall which is not taken up by the arcade: some distance up the wall is a semi-hexagonal string-course, and another one of different form below; the appearance is quite that of an external wall, which this, no doubt, was till the late Decorated period.

There are two elaborate Elizabethan tombs in this aisle. That against the north wall is to the memory of Sir George Bromley, who died in 1588, and his wife: they wear the usual Elizabethan costume, and the lady has the Mary Queen of Scots cap. The figures have been mutilated, especially those of the children below. The other tomb has a very elaborate canopy with Roman-Corinthian columns and Classical ornaments: it is that of Sir Edward Bromley, who died in 1626, and his wife, Margaret Lowe: the knight has legal costume, and his wife the usual ruffs of the period. Between these monuments is an incised slab to the memory of John de Worfield. The surface is a good deal worn, and it is impossible to make out some of the detail. There seems to be another name after "John." The date does not appear, but, judging by the lettering, we should suppose it to be some time in the 15th century. It is evidently the tomb of a priest, for we can make out the chasuble, the maniple hanging from the left arm, and the apparel of the alb near the feet.

There is an old chest with some intricate iron-work.

THE SOUTH AISLE

has four arches separating it from the nave. The eastern one, which has already been referred to, has the wave and sunk quarter-round mouldings. The other arches with their mouldings should be carefully compared with those in the north aisle. It would appear that the southern arcade was probably built a short time before the northern, for, though late Decorated, it is not quite so late as that opposite. On the south we have the scroll moulding to the abacus, and a base which is not quite of the bell-shape: the flat under edge is the same, as may be felt, where the work has not been renewed. The hood-mouldings in both cases are hollowed, the terminations on the south side being heads in some cases and foliage in others. The north wall of this aisle, like the south wall of the north aisle, was originally external; but there is this difference, that the north aisle as it now stands was apparently built in late Decorated times, whereas the south aisle originally had its west wall immediately west of the arcade, and was afterwards lengthened to meet the tower in the early Perpendicular period. This is shewn by the late Decorated window still remaining in the wall, west of the arcade.

I will refer later to the windows, but the beautiful glass in the east window of the aisle must be observed from the inside. It has been considerably restored, but a good deal of the old Decorated glass remains. It may be of some interest to point out that the early date is revealed, among other signs, by the low mitre worn by one of the figures, and by the absence of any mark of the iris of the eye; the natural foliage and the general character of the colouring and drawing shew that the glass is of the Decorated period. It would appear from the *Ecclesiologist* for December, 1846, that this glass was at that time in the east window of the *north* aisle.

The font is Perpendicular and has panelling, ornamental cusps, and quatrefoils with square leaves.

Some of the original moulding remains on the south door, with a sunk quarter-round similar to that used in other parts of the church.

An alms box has the inscription "BESURE AS YOU REMEMBER THE POOR 1683."

The moulding on the tower arch is of early Perpendicular character, and there are good four-leaf flowers on the capitals: the screen is rather like that across the chancel arch.

THE EXTERIOR.

Between the modern porch and the tower is a very remarkable small window. It has no tracery, but two lancet lights under a containing arch, and is clearly of Early English date. It is so like a belfry window that, with other evidence to be referred to shortly, it seems to shew that there was an Early English tower before the present one was built. Its present position is certainly not the original one; indeed the writer in the *Ecclesiologist*, already quoted, speaks of it as being above the Decorated window in the north wall of the south aisle.

The noble tower and spire of this church form a very prominent object for miles round. The tower is 80 feet high and the spire 120 feet. They are Perpendicular, but early in the style (see Plate XII.). The upper windows of the tower have tracery quite of Decorated character, but the date is revealed by the hollowed hood-mouldings. Underneath, on the north and south sides, are square-headed windows: the west window has been renewed, but the dripstone is original. The buttresses have bell-shaped basement mouldings.

The appearance of the north side of the tower is most interesting. High up there is a semi-hexagonal string-course, stopping a short distance beyond the west wall of the nave. Below this is a peculiar mark in the masonry, and at the bottom it will be noticed, behind some bushes, that the basement moulding of the nave is *continued a little way along the tower*

WORFIELD

wall, and does not fit in with the basement moulding of most of the tower. These signs shew very clearly that a portion of the north tower wall is earlier than the rest, and this is part of the evidence I have relied on in stating that there was a tower here in Early English days. The other proofs are the small belfry window already mentioned, and the character of the north tower wall inside the nave.

On the west wall of the nave is an early roll string-course, no doubt Early English. The west window has been renewed. About here the late Decorated string-course begins: the buttress looks modern. The west window of the north aisle is flowing Decorated, late in the style, as is shewn by the hood-moulding and finial. The character of the windows and base-ment mouldings on the north side is rather affected by the slope of the ground. The tracery, heads, and plain hood-mouldings are chiefly original. The window at the east end of the north aisle is very fine: all the tracery is original, though some of the mouldings are partly decayed. The arrangement of the buttresses at the east corner of both aisles is very peculiar (see Plan).

The chancel has been considerably restored, and the organ chamber on the north side is modern.

The east window of the south aisle is a beautiful early Decorated example. It is of three lights, the mullions simply crossing one another without cusps (see Plate XII.). Curiously enough the hood-moulding is the same as that over the west window of the north aisle, and must have been added some time after the tracery, as it is clearly late Decorated if not Perpendicular. The explanation may be that this window was moved from some other part of the church, when the extensive alterations took place in the latter part of the 14th century. The south windows of the aisle have been renewed, but parts of the original quarter-round mouldings remain in the jambs. The porch is modern.

The churchyard cross has been restored, but I cannot say if the old form has been reproduced.

The communion plate is modern. The parish register commences in the year 1562. We find that in this year the rood loft was taken down and the "altar stones" carried away.

The Hundred

of

Munslow.

Abdon.

St. Margaret.

ABDON chapel existed in the 12th century, for we find that it was assigned to the Abbey of Shrewsbury about the year 1138. No part of the present small building can be proved to be of this date, but part of the walls may have been built thus early, especially of the nave, which has thicker walls than the chancel.

The church was considerably altered some years ago. An extension was made to the nave at the west end: the junction with the old masonry can be plainly seen on the north side outside the church. At the same time the bell gable was rebuilt, and windows inserted, two on the north side and one on the south. The east window is also modern, and the only original window in the church is that on the south side of the chancel. This is a very good example of the early Decorated period, consisting of two trefoil sub-arches with a trefoil in the head. West of this is a plain niche in the wall, which has presumably been a piscina, but there are no remains of a drain.

The collar roof is a very plain one, probably of the late Perpendicular period, and was no doubt erected at the same time as the truss which separates the nave from the chancel: this has wooden supports underneath, between two of which is a piece of wood like a depressed arch.

The font is round, with heavy roll mouldings, and seems to belong to the Early English period.

The only door, on the south side, has a plain pointed arch and the sunk quarter-round moulding. It is therefore brobably of the 14th century, to which period the porch with its trussed-rafter roof may belong but there is no way of ascertaining precisely.

The parish register commences with the year 1554, but is imperfect till 1650.

Acton Scott.

St. Margaret.

THIS church is beautifully situated, some 700 feet above the sea. The churchyard, which contains some splendid yew trees, commands a most extensive view. The building itself is most disappointing, for it has been thoroughly modernised. We read of a church here as early as 1291, and the present building is no doubt ancient: the walls are very thick, especially those of the tower. There is, however, no detail of any interest. The roofs of nave and chancel; the south doorway of the chancel, with its broadly-hollowed hood-moulding; the south window of the nave, and some of the tower windows may be late Perpendicular, but nearly everything else is modern. In the east wall are three lancets, with detached, banded shafts inside, made of iron. On the north side of the nave is a transept, entered by a broad arch of Perpendicular form. A little knowledge of architecture will shew that this transept, with its ornamented ceiling and its windows, is modern Gothic, belonging no doubt to the early part of the century. The monuments to the family of the lord of the manor were placed in the chancel during the 18th century, but from the year 1819 onwards they have been placed in the transept. It seems evident then from this fact, and from the character of the architecture, that the transept was built and that the other alterations took place at the very beginning of the Gothic Revival, when the knowledge of mediæval architecture was somewhat confused. In this connection, the window in the north wall which lights the gallery should be noticed. It is evidently too high up to be an original window: it is also clear from its form—a good cusped single light—that it was not inserted in the 17th or 18th centuries, when most church galleries were erected. It is therefore evident that it must be referred to the early part of this century, when galleries were still in vogue, and when mediæval forms were being revived. The other work of this period seems to include the font, the pulpit and reading desk, and the elaborate screen, dividing the nave from the chancel. All this "restoration" and addition was very well done considering the period, but the result cannot now be regarded with satisfaction.

One of the tombs in the chancel already referred to is an

elaborate monument with four Doric pillars, supporting a pediment. It commemorates Edward Acton, Esq., second son of Sir Edward Acton, Bart., of Aldenham, who died in 1747. Near this is a small late brass to the memory of Elizabeth Mytton, who died in 1571 : there are representations of this lady and her husband, Thomas Mytton, and of nine sons and two daughters.

The south door is plain, and is approached through a porch, which has a round arch and classical mouldings, and was built in the year 1722. The tower is not quite due west of the nave : its windows are either late Perpendicular or of the early Revival period.

The parish register dates from the year 1670.

Ashford Bowdler.

St. Andrew.

THIS is a small church in a picturesque situation on the banks of the river Teme: it consists of chancel, nave, and small wooden turret and spire at the west end. The chancel and nave are evidently Norman, for there are blocked round-arched doorways on the north and south sides of the nave, and in the chancel there is a charming little Norman window on the north side, deeply splayed inwards.

The other windows of the church have no special interest. The east window, and one on the north and south sides of the nave, have lost their tracery and mullions, and another on the north side has been converted in modern times into a two-light window without tracery. Opposite the Norman window is a small opening, the date of which cannot well be determined: it is pointed on the outside and square-headed within. The west window is modern, as are the font, the south door and porch, and the small but well proportioned wooden turret and broach spire.

The chancel is simply a continuation of the nave, being separated from it merely by a plain tie-beam truss in the roof. The rest of the roof is hidden by a plaster ceiling.

The old "three decker" arrangement of the pulpit and reading desk is here preserved. The communion table is placed between the pulpit on one side and a pew on the other.

The parish register dates back to 1604.

Ashford Carbonell.

St. Mary.

IN mediæval times this parish seems to have constituted, with the adjoining one of Little Hereford, in Herefordshire, a Peculiar, and until quite recently these two parishes were a consolidated benefice. The church is a most interesting one and well worthy of examination. A small building, consisting of nave and chancel, seems to have been built in the Norman period. Later, but still in Norman times, the chancel was lengthened. In the 13th century the nave was added to, and the west window is of Early English form. Several windows were inserted in the Decorated period. The wooden turret at the west end, and the roof of the nave, are later. A good porch has recently been built on the south side, and there is some very good modern woodwork. The restoration took place in 1882-3, under the direction of Mr. Christian.

The most remarkable feature of this church is the character of the east windows. There are two deeply-splayed, round-headed Norman lights, and above these a pointed oval window, like the *vesica piscis* (see Fig. 7).

Fig. 7.

As is well known, this was a symbolical form, which succeeded, and had the same meaning as the early Christian symbol of the fish,—this latter being used because the Greek word for fish contained the initials of the names and titles of our Lord.   It is very interesting to note the distinct form of the pointed arch in Norman work, though of the latter part of the period. Of course the pointed *arch* occurs now and then as early as the middle of the 12th century, or even before, but it is very rare to have a pointed *window* before the Transitional period.   I think this must be one of the earliest instances of the use of the *vesica piscis* in building, for, though this form is often portrayed in Anglo-Saxon manuscripts, it is not generally seen as an *architectural* member till the very end of the 12th century or later.   Though we need not subscribe to Bloxam's opinion that this form had " weight towards originating and determining the adoption of the pointed arch," it is certainly most interesting to find it in this little country church, in the midst of work which is round-arched and Norman.   The late Mr. J. H. Parker, C.B., writing to the present vicar of the parish, said,—" The very remarkable east end of your church   .   .   .   I believe to be quite unique, at least I have never seen one like it, and I have seen more of our Mediæval Churches than most people have.   .   .   .   .   It is rather difficult to tell the exact date of it, the two lower windows by themselves would be of the 11th century, but it is hardly probable the vesica can be so early."   When Mr. Parker wrote this letter it was not known that the chancel had been extended : foundations of an earlier east wall were discovered some weeks afterwards.   The present wall no doubt belongs to the latter part of the Norman period, and not to the 11th century.   It will be noticed that some of the stones used to form these windows are not original.   Indeed, till the recent restoration of the church, the ancient form of the east end was very much hidden, and the only east *window* was the square-headed double light, which is now placed in the south wall at the west end of the chancel.   Fortunately, however, when this window was inserted at the east, in the 14th or 15th century, the stone-work of the old windows was not entirely removed, and enough remained to shew precisely the old form, so that, though some of the stonework has been renewed, we may rely on the form of the east end which is now shewn being exactly that given to it in the latter part of the Norman period.   The chancel roof is modern and succeeded one of similar form, which, however, had a tie-beam across the east wall. The removal of this was a great improvement, but the other tie-beams still spoil the appearance of the *vesica piscis* from the nave, and one regrets that a collar roof was not substituted for the old one.

There are three other Norman windows in the chancel, all well proportioned and deeply splayed.   On the south side are the square-headed window already referred to, and another of similar form : these may be

Decorated or Perpendicular. There is an aumbry at the north-east of the chancel, and, on the opposite side, a square-headed recess, which was, I suppose, a piscina, but there is now no basin. Another aumbry will be noticed in the north wall under one of the Norman windows. This is evidence to shew that the original chancel was only a part of the present one: there can be little doubt of this, as foundations have been discovered in the church, considerably to the west of the present east wall. An ancient monumental slab lies in the north-east corner of the chancel.

The chancel arch is a very plain Norman example, with square abaci, moulded in the usual manner.

The nave has several interesting windows. On either side is a Norman light, like those in the chancel, and also an early Decorated two-light window with a quatrefoil in the head. The quatrefoil on the south side has the original glass, natural leaves being represented. The moulding of this window, and also of some of the others, should be noticed. The stone-work was evidently cut to receive shutters, and some of the iron hooks still remain. Now this is a common feature of low-side windows, but the reason for them can hardly have been the same here. The most probable explanation of this is that the windows were brought from some domestic building, where the practice of having shutters to the lower parts of windows was a common one. On the sill of this south-eastern window of the nave a basin is cut, which was of course used as a piscina. Further west is the only modern window in the church. Foundations have recently been discovered, which shew that the original west wall of the nave was inside the present building. The extension evidently took place in the 13th century, as is shewn by the good Early English lancet in the west wall. The font may be Norman: it is circular and perfectly plain, resting on modern shafts. The roof is Perpendicular, of a peculiar form: one truss has a collar and a tie-beam, and the next a collar and hammer-beams. These hammer-beams do not support struts and braces, as is usual, and are of very little use, the weight of the roof resting entirely on the points where the hammer-beams join the cornice. We may perhaps refer the roof to the beginning of the 15th century, when hammer-beams were coming into fashion, but when possibly their principles were not thoroughly understood by builders of small churches. The pulpit is modern and is beautifully carved.

The south door is Norman, and has a plain tympanum of stone. The priest's door in the chancel and the blocked door on the north side of the nave both have signs of *late* Norman work about them. The former has the abacus slightly rounded instead of perfectly square, and the latter has an ornament which was the forerunner of the dog tooth of the Early English style. Now it is quite evident that the priest's door could not have existed in the original small chancel, for it would have been at the extreme east of it. This door then was inserted when the extension of the chancel took place. The architectural character shews that the north doorway was built at the same time—the latter part of the Norman period. The original small church, which may have been erected in the 11th century or early in the 12th, appears to have had only one door, that now entered through the porch.

On both sides of the nave will be noticed, from the outside, the remains of beams lower than the roof: this shews us the position of the roof which preceded the present one.

Over the Decorated window on the south side is a hood-moulding, with slight ogee curves at the top: it is evidently early in the period, as the scroll moulding is combined with a deep undercutting. The hood of the west window has a narrow hollow, as we should expect in the Early English style. The plinth of the west wall has a heavy roll string-course, and a slope below— a common form in Early English work, though sometimes occurring in Norman. The wooden bell-turret has no special interest or beauty, but is very characteristic of small Shropshire churches.

This parish possesses an Elizabethan chalice. The register dates back to 1653.

Broadstone.

Dedication unknown.

HAVE been unable to find any early reference to Broadstone as a chapelry of Munslow, but a small building there has been used as a place of worship for a long period. Till about the year 1843 this was used as a farm building, and service was held only twice a year, on Christmas Day and Good Friday, but since then it has been entirely devoted to its original purpose. There is very little architectural interest in the church. It is a small oblong building, with a bell gable at the west end. The windows all appear to be modern: the font seems to have been presented in 1843. There is some 17th century carving on the pulpit and communion table.

Bromfield.

St. Mary.

ROMFIELD was an important place, ecclesiastically, at an early period. In the reign of Edward the Confessor, it possessed a collegiate foundation consisting of twelve secular canons, without any ostensible head. This constitution appears to have been changed early in the Norman period, for we read of a certain Osbert, Prior of Bromfield in 1115. It appears that the secular canons became regulars about this time, and we find that in 1155 they affiliated themselves to the important Benedictine abbey of St. Peter at Gloucester. Unfortunately little else is known of the history of this priory.

Eyton states, in the *Antiquities of Shropshire*, that the parish church was probably, but not certainly, distinct from the priory. It is known that the Saxon parish of Bromfield was very extensive, including Ludford and Halford, and very possibly several other places and even Ludlow itself. The church of St. Mary is mentioned in Domesday Book. The first vicar, whose name is known, is Thomas de Bromfeud, incumbent in 1285.

We must now enquire how far the history of the priory and parish church is illustrated and supplemented by the architecture of the present building.

There are no remains to lead us to suppose that there were two separate buildings, but I think we shall see that it is highly probable that part of the church was used for the priory and part as the parish church. It will be at once noticed that there are indications of Norman work. These seem to shew pretty clearly that the church was originally cruciform, consisting of nave, without aisles; chancel, and transepts, with central tower. We may refer this to the early Norman period, but scarcely, I think, to the time of Edward the Confessor.

About the end of the 12th century the tower appears to have fallen down and to have partially destroyed the chancel and north transept, which were not rebuilt, in consequence, no doubt, of the insecure nature of the foundations, close to the bank of the river Onny. The date I have named for this catastrophe may be placed a little earlier, but cannot be later,

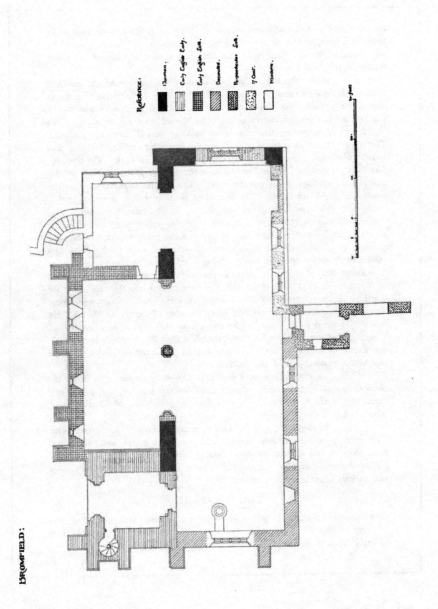

BROMFIELD:

Reference:
Norman.
Early English Early.
Early English Late.
Decorated.
Perpendicular Early.
17 Cent.
Modern.

for the tower at the north-west corner of the church must have been built about this time, and it is not likely that it would have been erected while the central tower was standing. The aisle to the nave was added about the middle of the 13th century.

After the fall of the central tower the portion of the building used by the monks must have been reduced to the south transept, and the part formerly under the tower, now the chancel. The parishioners would worship in the nave, afterwards enlarged by the addition of an aisle. This is, of course, supposing that the same building served for both purposes. That this was the case seems almost certain from the way the building was treated, when the Dissolution of the priory took place in 1538. The property was then granted to Charles Foxe, who seems to have proceeded to fit up the conventual buildings as his private house. The remains of this appear on the south side (see Plate XIV.). The important point to notice, however, is that this private house *included the present chancel*; for the ruins are directly connected with the church, there is a window of the period, now blocked, in the east wall, and, above all, high up in the eastern gable, is another blocked window, which shews quite plainly that the chancel was divided into two stories, the upper one, no doubt, being used as a bedroom! Now the Dissolution caused no interruption in the succession of vicars: presentations were made in 1534 and 1539, and the nave was evidently still used for worship. It seems very unlikely, however, that Mr. Charles Foxe would have dared to desecrate the chancel if it had been part of the parish church. He evidently treated it as a part of the conventual buildings, over which he had a legal if not a moral right. I think, therefore, that this evidence leaves little doubt that in mediæval times the parish used the nave and aisles, and the monks the eastern part of the building.

In 1577 a new roof was placed over the nave. In 1658 the chancel appears to have been restored to its original purpose, and a new roof erected by Richard Herbert, of Oakly Park, a descendant of Charles Foxe, who in 1672 caused the chancel to be painted throughout.

In 1889—1890 the church was restored by Mr. C. Hodgson Fowler. The archway, which formerly opened into a north transept, and which had been blocked, was opened out, and a vestry and organ chamber added. The plaster was removed from the roof of the nave, the western gallery taken away and various other alterations made.

THE CHANCEL,

as before mentioned, is only a portion of the original eastern part of the building. The old chancel arch can be plainly seen in the east wall; it is of early Norman character, and the carving on the capitals is very quaint.

It scarcely looks capable of sustaining a tower, and indeed, if my explanation is correct, it failed to do so for any length of time, and it shews evidence of being overloaded in its present depressed state. The piscina in the east wall should be carefully noticed: it has a trefoil head, such as might be used in the Early English period, and its form does not clash with the statement already made that the tower fell down, and that this wall was built about the end of the 12th century. The arch which opened into the north transept, is of the same early period as the eastern arch, but is plainer, having square moulding and no ornament on the capitals. The southern arch no longer exists, though it is probable that there was a south transept of the same size as the north. At any rate it is quite evident that the south wall of the chancel is not original, for it is much nearer the eastern arch than the north wall is; the awkward position of this arch is very soon noticed on entering the church. When, therefore, was this south wall built and the transept removed? There is scarcely enough evidence to decide the point. At first one might suppose that it was at the same time as the east wall, but the monks can scarcely have had room enough in the present chancel, and the piscina would probably not have been placed in the east wall if there had been a south wall conveniently near. The canopy in the wall is of the 14th century, but this may have been removed from the transept and rebuilt here, when the chancel was restored to the church by Richard Herbert, who may have considered it a dignified covering for the remains of his ancestor, Charles Foxe. The feathering of this canopy is very beautiful, and the scroll and roll and fillet mouldings are rich; the hood-moulding is of the scroll form and ends with curious representations of heads. Under the canopy are some ancient tiles, part of an incised slab with a fleur-de-lis ornament, some chevron carving, and the arms of Charles Foxe and Elizabeth Crosby, his first wife. The position of the stone bearing the arms has not been changed recently, but the other fragments were found in various parts of the church and placed here. Above are three modern lights of Decorated form, which replaced a debased window at the restoration.

The panelling on the walls has the linen pattern: a good deal of the woodwork used in the church and vestry was taken from the old pews. The triptych was designed by Mr. Fowler, and executed in 1890. There was no doubt a central tower here originally, but the western arch, like the southern, has disappeared. The chancel is separated from the nave by a screen, which, like the other modern woodwork in the church is extremely good.

The wonderful painted ceiling (see Plate XIII.) has been described as "the best specimen of the worst period of ecclesiastical art." The whole chancel was painted in 1672, at the expense of Richard Herbert, but the

BROMFIELD.

ceiling alone survives. The vicar and architect have actually been blamed for retaining this at the restoration. They are to be heartily congratulated on having done so. The painting may not be a great work of art, it may not be "Gothic," but it was no doubt the best which could be done at the time, and it would have been a thousand pities to have removed a specimen of the period which is at once characteristic and unique. It is true that the ceiling almost hides the roof above, but the nave is covered by a similar roof, partly of the same period, and ceilings of this kind are very much rarer than roofs. The coats of arms have been made out to be those of the Foxe, Newton, Burnell, Galton, Herbert, Corbett, and other families.

THE NAVE

has a good collar-braced roof. The four west trusses are of the date 1577, which is carved on every corbel : one of the collars has the inscription

This ruffe was made by me
John gethi 1577

The arms represented are those of the Foxe, Leighton, Stoke, Stevinton, and Crosby families. The eastern part of the roof is of almost exactly the same form but of later date : one of the collars (see Plate XIII.) has the inscription

namhtimS drahciR 1658 William Woodall

The south wall has two modern windows with Decorated tracery : between these is a large representation of the royal arms, with the inscription

C R
1670

Further west is a square-head recess, which is shewn as a window in the view in Eyton's *Antiquities* : the same view has a large round-headed window, east of this, but there are no signs of it now.

The west wall has a large modern window of four lights, with reticulated tracery : this replaced a three-light window of the same form, which was not in the centre of the gable ; the tracery of this is preserved in the churchyard with some other fragments.

There are signs of a round-headed window in the north wall, which shews that the Norman church extended thus far at least. The stoup is Early English, as is also the font, which is circular and has the hollow moulding, characteristic of the period, but not very pronounced in this case. The pulpit was made by a local joiner, using some Jacobean panels, elaborately carved with scenes in the life of our Lord. The lectern is copied from one in Southwell minster.

THE AISLE

is separated from the nave by a beautiful arcade. It consists of only two bays, but the arches are so bold and well-proportioned, and the moulding of the capitals and bases so good, that the effect is most striking.

Fig. 8 shews a section of the western respond. An examination of this will shew that the probable date of the arcade is circa 1250: the abacus and neck have the scroll moulding, shewing the approach of the Decorated style, but the base has the characteristic water-rim of the Early English, and the lowest roll round underneath. The central column, which is round and massive, has a simple capital, but the base is the same except that the lowest roll is filleted. The base of the eastern respond has been renewed to match the one shewn in Fig. 8: the capital has a beautiful row of the dog-tooth ornament, nearly all being original (see Plate XIII.). All the plinths are octagonal, another sign that the work is not of the *early* part of the 13th century. The arcade has no hood-moulding on the north side, but on the south is one, under-cut, and having the characteristic mask ornament used at the terminations.

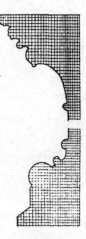

Fig. 8.

The west wall has clear indications that it was once external on the east side. There are remains of a window high up, and at the bottom is a basement moulding, consisting of a semi-hexagonal string-course and a slope below. There is another string-course above, of the same form but smaller. We shall see presently that this corresponds very well with the other architectural features of the tower.

There are four lancets in the north wall, and underneath the heavy roll string-course, so often seen in the Early English style. The windows are filled with stained glass, which, like the rest of the glass in the church, is by Mr. C. E. Kempe. The effect of colour is, as we should expect from this artist, rich and restful.

The east window is modern. Against the east wall, as at the opposite end of the aisle, are various architectural fragments, discovered when the church was restored. By the vestry door is what must have been, I think, a piscina and not a stoup. It is of Norman character and therefore rare: it is not unlike that of Towersey, figured in the *Glossary of Architecture.* The roof is like that part in the nave dated 1658. The vestry contains a list of the priors and vicars, so far as they have been ascertained.

THE TOWER

is at the north-west corner of the church, and the church is entered through

BROMFIELD.

it. The inner doorway is shewn in Fig. 9. It is a simple but very bold and

Fig. 9.

effective composition. The chief moulding is a large roll and fillet, continued down the jambs. The capitals have beautiful stiff-leaf foliage, scarcely of the developed Early English form. The bases have slight water-rims. The hood-moulding is under-cut: the western termination is composed of stiff-leaf foliage; the eastern one is a poor plaster parody, stuck on when the church was "restored" in 1844. The doorway to the staircase has an under-cut hood-moulding. A semi-hexagonal string-course appears on the east and west walls.

The outer doorway is a fine large arch. The hood-moulding is semi-hexagonal, as it might have been in Norman times, and the abaci are almost of Norman character. The west capital has undeveloped stiff-leaf foliage. The opposite one has rosettes: some of these have been judiciously restored, and one is not deceived as to what is new and what is old.

It will be seen that the architectural evidence of this part fits in with what we have already observed on the west wall of the aisle, and shews us that the tower was built in the Transition period, between Norman and Early English, late in the 12th century or early in the 13th. The rest of the tower shews the same style, with the slightly projecting buttresses, the string-courses, and the windows—two lancets under one head and no tracery. The upper part of the tower, as is often the case, is much later, having been added in the Perpendicular period.

THE EXTERIOR

view is striking, and the situation of the church, on a peninsula between the rivers Teme and Onny, is most picturesque.

The north wall of the aisle had to be partly rebuilt at the restoration. The two western lancets are original, though having a few new stones : the other two are modern and replaced a square-headed window. There is a row of good bold corbels supporting the roof.

The most striking feature on the south side is the remains of Mr. Charles Foxe's house (see Plate XIV.). Whether these walls formed part of the conventual buildings or not is difficult to say : all the detail is late Perpendicular. The buttress against the south wall of the chancel is puzzling at first sight, for it has the appearance of Norman work, and it has already been shewn that this wall is later. I have ascertained, however, that the buttress is modern, though built chiefly of old stones.

The east wall has the late Perpendicular window already referred to, and the bedroom window above ! Both of these are now blocked. The junction of the Norman stone-work with the later wall built across the old chancel arch can be plainly seen. On the north side there are still some remains of the east wall of the transept. This wall was evidently not a buttress, though at first sight it might be mistaken for one.

The parish possesses a chalice dated 1672 : the rest of the communion plate is later. The register commences with the year 1559.

Cardington.

St. James.

THE parish of Cardington has been an extensive one since
Anglo-Saxon days. Corbet Anderson, in his *Shropshire: its
early history and antiquities*, states that the church was held
by the Templars, who had the rectory, as well as the advowson
of the vicarage. It has been thought that part of the present
building existed before the Conquest, but I think there is no
part of it which can be safely referred to this early period.
Norman remains, however, there are, which shew us that in
the 12th century there was a church here with nave, and no
doubt chancel as well.

In the Early English period the old chancel appears
to have been removed, and a larger one erected. The western
tower was also built at the same time. Several windows were
inserted in the 14th century, but there is little or no Perpendicular work.

The church was restored about 1869, when an ugly partition,
which almost shut off the nave from the chancel, was removed. The tracery
of some of the windows was renewed, a new font was erected and various
minor alterations were carried out.

THE CHANCEL

is separated from the nave by modern masonry, supporting an ornamental
truss in the roof. The east window has three lights of lancet shape, such
as was often used in the latter part of the Early English period.

The old priest's door is in the *north* wall, where can also be
seen an aumbry and two Early English windows, one of which is a single
lancet, and the other not unlike the east window, but with two lights only.

The windows in the south wall are similar to those in the north.
There is an elaborate tomb to the memory of William Leighton, of Plashe, Esq.,
Chief Justice of North Wales, who died in 1607. The Elizabethan costume
is worn, and there are representations of three sons and four daughters, besides
one child who died in infancy. Further west, and underneath the two-light
window, is a very beautiful cinque-foiled double piscina, with deeply cut basins.
This was discovered behind the tomb, when the church was restored, and
removed to its present position: it is still used.

The roof has tie and collar beams, and quatrefoils between the purlins. That of

THE NAVE

is similar, but has braces instead of quatrefoils. The pulpit has some very strange and inexplicable devices carved upon it: one of them is original, and the others copied. The pews retain their old Elizabethan woodwork, altered to suit modern ideas: various initials are carved upon them, and the names of some of the townships in the parish.

The tracery of the Decorated window in the north wall has been renewed. Further west is a Norman splayed window, and a blocked door.

In the south wall are three Decorated windows; the two eastern ones are formed chiefly of original stonework. There is also a Norman window, similar and opposite to that on the north side.

The tower arch is lofty and well-proportioned. The mouldings are effective, particularly the bold roll and fillet. The west window is a long lancet, near which is a quaint inscription, describing the duties of the bell-ringers. The font is modern.

THE EXTERIOR.

The south doorway has been considerably restored. The arch is semi-circular, and one of the capitals has foliage, which is almost stiff-leaf. The stonework on the west side is considerably damaged. The parish clerk tells me it was done some fifty years ago by a tombstone engraver, who found this to be a convenient place for sharpening his instruments. The same enterprising person, for the same purpose, was in the habit of removing pieces of stone from the elaborate tomb in the chancel. It is a strange thought that the Jacobean monument should be mutilated to whet the chisel of the Victorian monument carver. The south door itself bears the date 1648. The porch was built in 1639, and is a good example of Renaissance woodwork.

The remains of a remarkable round arch in the south wall deserve attention. They are evidently Norman; the abaci are square, and one capital is left with a simple volute carved upon it. This arch is now blocked, and cut into by one of the 14th century windows already referred to. It is a little difficult to say what it was used for. The width is about the same as that of the main doorway, but the height is greater. It seems to be hardly large enough for the entrance into a chapel or transept, and I suppose it must have been a doorway. A little observation will shew that all the Norman remains in this church are higher in the wall than we should expect. Is it possible that there may have been a crypt to the building, which was removed and the floor of the nave lowered at a later period? If so, the arch we are considering would no longer be convenient as an entrance to the church, and

another one would be erected. This was certainly done; for the main doorway is at a lower level than this blocked one, and is evidently later, as the
character of the foliage shews. I should put it down to the Transition period,
and the small lancet east of it probably to the same time. Of course I do
not pretend that there is absolute proof of the former existence of a crypt,
but the assumption that there was explains a good deal. It would be
interesting to test how far the walls go down.

It will be observed that the masonry of the chancel is quite
different from that of the nave: there is a basement moulding of Early
English character. I cannot say what the square recess over the east
window was for: it bears the date 1863, but is no doubt more ancient than
that.

In the north wall of the nave there are indications of a round
arch in exactly the same position as that in the south wall. This arch however
was much smaller: indeed the appearance of the masonry is such that it
is very doubtful whether the arch was ever pierced as an entrance. Further
west is a doorway, which has been blocked in modern times. The old form
of it is not apparent, for the head is now composed of what seems to have
been a mill-stone.

The lower part of the tower is Early English: the windows
have two lancets under one head, and no tracery. The upper part is either
late Decorated or Perpendicular.

The parish register dates back to 1598.

Church Stretton.

St. Lawrence.

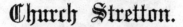

THIS is a Saxon foundation, and Domesday speaks of the church of Stretton, and of a resident priest there.

The present building dates from Norman times, the nave being of that period. Considerable alterations took place at the end of the 12th century, or very early in the 13th : a central tower and transepts were built, and the chancel, which up to that time had doubtless been in the position of the tower, placed further east.

In the 14th century some windows may have been inserted, and in the Perpendicular period a considerable addition was made to the tower.

In the year 1619 some alterations, which will presently be referred to, were probably made. In 1831 a porch, now used as a vestry, was built south of the nave, and, between the years 1867 and 1883, west aisles were added to the transepts, an organ chamber built north of the chancel, and the church generally " restored."

THE INTERIOR.

The view in Eyton's *Antiquities* shews an east window of Decorated character, but the present window has modern Perpendicular tracery and mouldings. The other windows and the doorway I will refer to shortly. There is some fine Jacobean carved woodwork at the east end : this did not belong to the church originally, but was presented by a former rector, early in this century. The shouldered arch near the organ appears to have been an entrance to the tower staircase before the organ-chamber was built.

The central tower is supported by four arches, which exhibit a mixture of Norman and Early English characteristics. The abaci are square, and moulded in the usual Norman manner, but the arches are pointed ; fillets are used on the columns, water-hollows on the bases, and, on one of the capitals, foliage is carved, quite of the stiff-leaf type. This foliage is on the eastern respond of the south arch (see Fig. 10). It will be observed that the foliage

Fig. 10.

on the south side of the capital is quite Early English in character.   That
which goes round the capital is not so fully developed, and is often seen in
Transitional work.   The heads are beautifully carved, and those on the
eastern respond of the north arch are equally good.   The opposite
responds and all the capitals of the east and west arches have ornamental
volutes.   The columns of the north and south arches terminate some distance
from the floor.   The bases of the columns of the eastern arch have been
renewed, but the original ones with the water-rims will be observed on the
opposite side of the tower: the plinths are square.   There are lancet windows
in the transepts, and, on the whole, Early English characteristics rather pre-
dominate over Norman in the part of the building built at this time, and we
may therefore refer it to the very end of the 12th or the very early part of
the 13th century.

An original doorway of this Transition period remains on the
west side of the north transept.   It is now internal, in consequence of the
modern aisle on that side: this aisle has ornamentation of late 12th century
character, and a semi-circular arch to the nave.   The north wall has a window
with reticulated tracery, to be referred to presently, but the position of two
original lancet windows can be traced.

The large window in the south transept has been a good deal
renewed.   The arches of the aisle have similar ornaments to those on the
north side.

The roofs of chancel, nave, and north transept are of the trussed-rafter form. That of the nave is particularly fine, and may date back as far as the 13th century. The roof of the south transept is partly on the same principle, combined with collar-beams, and a tie-beam at the north end: it is ornamented with quatrefoils. The pulpit is modern, and to the memory of a former rector.

The old south doorway of the nave is now in the modern vestry. It is Norman and rather plain: the western capital is ornamented with volutes. On one side of the door is a Norman buttress. The font is octagonal, and dates from the Perpendicular period: it is ornamented with shields and square flowers. Near the font is some Jacobean carved woodwork, arranged there in 1885 from portions of an old oak pulpit, taken down in 1879.

THE EXTERIOR.

The buttresses at the end of the nave are joined together, and form a thickening of the wall at the corners. They are of course Norman, of the usual flat type. The west doorway is modern.

High up on the wall the date 1619 is carved, and it seems probable that we may refer the debased work in the church to this date. I am not sure that the west window and the large windows at the ends of the transepts were not inserted at this period. It is true that they are of Decorated form, but they are decidedly coarse, and there are many instances of "Jacobean Gothic" work, where Decorated tracery rather than Perpendicular is copied. This theory is strengthened if the hood-moulding of the south transept window has been renewed after the old pattern: it is certainly not Decorated. However, I should not like to say definitely that these windows were not inserted in the 14th century: all three have the double ogee of Decorated form, but coarsely worked, on the jambs. Perhaps the true explanation may be that they were put up in the 14th and repaired in the 17th century. It is evident that something was done to the church in 1619, and the work probably included the coarse hood-mouldings to windows on the north and south sides of the chancel. I think some of the windows themselves, namely the double lancets without cusps, may be referred to this period. They are almost too broad to be original 13th century insertions. The similar window in the south wall of the nave is more acutely pointed and may possibly be Early English.

The vestry bears the date 1831, and has a window of more or less Decorated appearance. The lancet window in the south transept aisle has some old stones, and was, I suppose, moved from the transept when the aisle was built. In the south-west corner of the chancel is a window in the position that a low side-window often occupies. It has a deep sill underneath

CHURCH STRETTON.

it inside, but there is no sign of a shutter, or of the wall being pierced under the present base of the window: it is difficult to assign a date to it. The square-headed window above is probably not mediæval. The south door-way of the chancel may well be the original one. It has the heavy roll moulding often used in the 13th century: the hood and that of the north doorway are of the same coarse character as that of the windows. The chancel walls slope slightly towards the bottom in a manner commonly seen in buildings of the period. The east wall bears the date 1819 below the window. The organ chamber has an imitation of Norman interlacing on its north side.

The most interesting doorway of the church is that, now blocked, in the north wall of the nave (see Plate XV.). It is clearly Norman, and has the usual semi-circular arch and square abaci. The wall is thicker round the doorway, which is once recessed. The abaci on the west side are carved with the rosette, cable, and round billet ornaments. The capitals opposite are not the original ones, but, curiously enough, have been replaced by a much later piece of stone, apparently a Perpendicular basement moulding, turned upside down! There are various fragments above the door, including a quaint representation of a human figure.

It will be observed that many of the details in this church are more curious than beautiful, but this remark does not refer to the central tower. The beautiful Transitional arches are quite the feature of the interior of the church, and the fine Perpendicular work above them is the most striking sight outside (see Plate XV.). The Transitional walls appear for some distance above the roof, but the whole of the upper part is Perpendicular. The ornamentation is rich and effective. The windows are cusped and pointed, under square heads. The gargoyles, unfortunately, are considerably decayed, but they are still unusually fine and grotesque. The upper part of the tower is rather narrower than the lower, and has slight diagonal buttresses at the corners. In the south-east buttress is a figure of the patron saint, St. Lawrence, with the usual accompaniment of the gridiron.

The parish register dates from 1662.

Clee St. Margaret.

St. Margaret.

THIS is a small church, dating back to the latter part of the Norman period. There are, as usual, later additions: two windows belong to the Decorated style, and there is woodwork of a later date. About 1872 the church was restored, and a vestry built on the north side of the nave.

I cannot say what reasons led the restorers of this church to place a lancet in the east wall. As the chancel is Norman, one would have expected a round-headed window. A sketch made by the Rev. J. Brooke in 1856 shews a debased square-headed window of two lights in this position. The north window of the chancel is evidently original, but the proportions are spoilt by the square head inside. Opposite to this is a somewhat rude two-light window of the Decorated period. The aumbry in the north wall has a door and is still used. There is some interesting woodwork. The chair within the rails is dated 1692, and one of the chancel seats has an inscription, shewing it to have been carved in 1639. The last three letters of this date are the wrong way round, though in the right order. The doors to the chancel have carving of Elizabethan character: they were made chiefly from an old chest.

The chancel arch is pointed, but has moulding more of Norman than of Early English appearance: in the middle of the hood-moulding is a modern head, which is very much out of keeping with the rest. On either side of this low arch is a large hagioscope.

The north and west windows of the nave have been renewed; that on the south can be the better observed from the outside. The pulpit is probably of the same date as the chancel seats. The font may be as old as the church: it is circular and plain, on a modern octagonal base. There are a number of very thick oak pews. These and the roofs of the chancel and nave may well be of the 14th century, though possibly of the 15th.

The porch is modern, but the south doorway is Norman and has a segmental arch: the rounded form of the abaci indicates a late date in the period. The door has some old ironwork upon it. The south window of the nave has lost its tracery, but the date can be ascertained by the moulding on the jambs, which is of three orders of the sunk chamfer, so characteristic of the Decorated period. The remains of the square-headed priest's door, now blocked, can be seen on the south side of the chancel. In the east and north walls of the chancel there is the most interesting feature of this church—the use of the herring-bone masonry. This, of course, was a common form in Roman work, and it is not very rare in early mediæval times. The wooden bell-turret is in a ruinous condition and is of no interest.

This parish possesses a chalice of early post-Reformation date. The register has a single entry of the year 1634, but is continuous only from 1660.

Cold Weston.

St. Mary.

THIS is the small parish church of one of the most sparsely populated parishes in the kingdom : the number of parishioners is only about 20. The building dates back to the late Norman period. There is a window of this date in the south wall of the chancel, but all the other windows are modern, with the exception of the east window, which has two lights under a square head, and is Perpendicular : this last has no tracery, its period being revealed by the hollowed mullion. The roof is collar-braced, and the chancel is separated from the nave by two queen-post trusses, placed near together. The font may belong to almost any style : it is plain and octagonal. The only doorway is on the north side : it is clearly Norman, with a round arch and the usual hood-moulding, but the latter part of the period is indicated by the corners of the square abaci being cut off, and by the ornaments at the ends of the chamfer which goes round the arch. The church was restored in 1876. A poor modern bell-gable of wood is now being replaced by one of stone. Two 18th century dates appear outside the building, at the east and west ends, but what they refer to is not very clear.

The parish register dates from the year 1690.

Culmington.

All Saints.

THE Rev. R. W. Eyton states that the first positive reference to the church of Culmington is between 1177 and 1185, but that it probably existed previously. I do not think that any part of the present building can be referred to the 12th century. It is chiefly Early English work, and both nave and chancel are doubtless of the 13th century. The lancet windows are remarkably acute, and begin to taper much lower down than is usual: there can be no doubt however that they are original. In the 14th century a tower was added at the west end, and a spire commenced, which has never been finished: there are also windows of this period. The vestry has been added in modern times, but very little "restoration" has lately taken place in the church, which is a very interesting example of the architecture of the two periods above named.

THE INTERIOR.

In the east wall are three lancets under one head: the hood-moulding seems to terminate in corbels of foliage, so far as one can make out; whitewash covers them, and hides the form.

The lancet window in the north wall of the chancel is now blocked. Underneath, and round the chancel and part of the nave, runs a heavy roll string-course, so characteristic of the Early English style. The doorway leading to the vestry is round-headed, and at first sight appears to be Norman; but there is no sure indication of early work about it, and I think it must be modern like the vestry itself.

In the south wall is a beautiful double piscina with a trefoil head: the hood-moulding is undercut in the 13th century manner, and the cusps terminate in trefoil leaves; the basins are not so deep as they often were at this period. Beyond is a lancet window, blocked, and a small recess, which may have been an aumbry. Farther west is a two-light Decorated window with reticulated tracery. Under this is a fine Decorated canopy: the ball-flower is used in profusion, and the whole is very effective. There is no sepulchral slab underneath, or anything to shew the original use of the canopy. West of this again is another blocked lancet.

The roof is rather a rough one. Two trusses near together mark the division of the chancel from the nave ; in the former the purlin braces are straight, and in the latter curved. The screen is rather poor work, and is less likely to be ancient than of the early Gothic Revival.

Near the pulpit was the staircase to the rood-loft. Further west is another Decorated window, and there are two lancets in the north wall opposite. The font is modern.

The date of the tower is indicated partly by the wave mouldings on the tower arch, which bulge very slightly in the Decorated manner. It must not be supposed that the lancet windows low down on the north and south sides indicate Early English work. Lancet windows were sometimes used in unimportant positions in the Decorated period, and these are not nearly so acute at the top as those in the 13th century part of the building. The west door is modern. A sketch made by the Rev. J. Brooke in 1856 shews a south porch, apparently of wood : this has now disappeared.

THE EXTERIOR

is chiefly remarkable for the unfinished spire of the 14th century. It is a broach spire, beginning very gracefully, but ending abruptly at about one-third of its proper height. The small pointed erection above, of wood and lead, forms a rather ludicrous finish. The water-spouts from this are arranged to combine the minimum of beauty with the maximum of damage to the stonework ! The buttresses at the west corners of the tower have the scroll moulding, again indicating the Decorated period.

It will be noticed that the stonework of some of the lancet windows of the church has been renewed, but the old form has evidently been preserved, as the internal splays shew.

On the south side, a thickening of the wall indicates the position of the staircase to the rood-loft. East of this, and below a blocked lancet, is a blocked low side-window, square and barred.

The hood-moulding over the east window is undercut in the Early English manner and terminates in heads. This part of the church appears to have had plaster put on in modern times, and the vulgar deception practised of making it appear like large stones.

The parish register commences with the year 1579.

Diddlebury, or Delbury.

St. Peter.

THE Rev. R. W. Eyton supposes that this church is of Saxon foundation, as it was among the first grants made by Earl Roger and his Countess Adeliza to the Abbey of Shrewsbury. This supposition is well borne out by the architecture of the present building; for the south wall of the nave and part of the tower are certainly Saxon. There is nothing to indicate whether this early building extended to the east of the nave, but a considerable chancel was evidently built in the Norman period. Towards the end of the 12th century the tower was partly rebuilt, and in the 13th a south aisle was added to the nave. Several windows were inserted in the 14th century, and possibly two in the 15th, that is if the two Perpendicular windows in the south aisle have been renewed on the old form.

The Cornewall chapel, so called, on the north side, seems to have been built early in the 17th century. It will be seen that this village church has examples of almost every style of English architecture, and it is well worth a visit.

Various repairs to the church were carried out in the years 1840, 1843, 1844. In 1860 the roof was renewed, and the south wall of the aisle rebuilt, and in 1884 the porch was erected and various minor alterations made.

THE INTERIOR.

There is no division between the chancel and the nave. The former is evidently an addition of the Norman period, and there are two windows of that character remaining, one in the south and one in the north wall. The east wall has the remains of two other round-headed windows. There were no doubt three, which were blocked when a three-light window was inserted in the Decorated period: this window has been renewed in recent times. There are good early Decorated windows in the north and south walls of the chancel. That on the north side has some of the original glass in the trefoil at the head of the window: it displays a representation of the Crucifixion, and the usual natural foliage of the period. The rear arch of this window has the characteristic sunk chamfer moulding, which is not used on the one opposite. There are two good Decorated canopies with the ball-flower ornament. The one on the north side was probably for an Easter sepulchre: it is well moulded with the scroll and other forms. The canopy on the south side is smaller and less elaborate :. it is evident from its appearance that the chancel floor has been raised ; this was done in 1884. There is a plain trefoil-headed piscina in the usual position : the basin has been renewed. The window west of the priest's door can scarcely be called a low side-window : it is square-headed and of doubtful date. Near this is a projecting corbel, which may have carried a rood beam.

On the north side two modern arches open into what is now a vestry and organ chamber. This is generally called the Cornewall chapel, but I doubt whether it was ever a chapel at all : it is probably post-Reformation. A brass commemorates one of the Baldwyn family, who died in 1614. The addition to the church probably took place about this time or a little earlier. It was used as the squire's pew by the Cornewall family, many of whom are buried here, including F. H. W. Cornewall, Bishop of Worcester, who died in 1831.

One of the most interesting features of the church is the masonry of the north wall of the nave. It is undoubtedly Saxon, and, on the inside, is composed of herring-bone work. This has recently been re-pointed, and looks far too modern. It is however original, and there is a thoroughly genuine Saxon window. It is high up in the wall, and splayed on the outside as well as within, in the manner peculiar to Saxon work. The glass of course is modern, and there appears to have been a shutter originally, as may be observed from the outside. East of this is a window which seems to have been Decorated, but it has been considerably renewed. Further east is a blocked Norman window, which is continued down in a peculiar way, forming a recess, the use of which it is difficult to understand. At the back of this is a rude carving, apparently of a Jesse tree. On the east jamb of the Decorated window just mentioned is another carved stone, evidently Saxon, and of the well-known interlacing character. West of the blocked Saxon doorway is a modern window of Decorated character. The nave roof was renewed in 1860, but the old wooden corbel heads were preserved.

The aisle is separated from the nave by an arcade of five bays. These are probably Early English, as the abaci are more or less undercut and the plinths are square, but the moulding is very poor. The columns are octagonal and so are the two western abaci, the others being round. The south wall was rebuilt in 1860, and the windows in it and the east wall of the aisle are of that period. That in the west wall is a single Decorated light, and has the sunk chamfer moulding. The font is octagonal and probably Decorated, with quatrefoils carved round it. The south door and porch are modern, the latter having been built in 1884, to replace one which was removed.

The tower is entered from the nave by a recessed arch of late 12th century date. The wall is more than five feet thick here and is evidently Saxon, as the herring-bone masonry on the north wall is continued on this. Higher up the wall is a Norman string-course, and above this the wall is considerably thinner. Near the roof will be observed a single light with cusps. This is no doubt Decorated, but the appearance of the arch on the west side rather suggests that it was originally Norman.

THE EXTERIOR

is even more interesting than the interior. The north wall has no herring-bone masonry visible, as on the inside, but it is Saxon, and the basement moulding is of that character, such as may be seen at the well known Saxon church at Worth, in Sussex. This moulding is continued along the tower wall and shews that there must have been a tower in Saxon times. The old Saxon door in the north wall is now blocked. It has the hood-moulding continued down the jambs, and of the characteristic square form without chamfers, which, however, are found on the abaci. The Saxon window has already been referred to. East of the Cornewall "chapel" are signs of a Norman window which were not visible from the inside.

On the south side the wall is thinner towards the east end. There is no apparent reason for this, as the chancel wall is evidently of one period throughout : there is nothing to correspond with it on the north side. The priest's door appears to be of the 13th century, but may be of the 14th. .

We have already seen that parts of the east and north walls of the tower are Saxon. The large arch in the west wall may possibly be of the same period, but it appears to be almost too large for a doorway and now acts as a sort of relieving arch to the smaller doorway below, which is later and of the same date as the eastern tower arch—the latter part of the 12th century. The tower has been patched and buttressed at various periods, and the south wall has been entirely rebuilt. There are Norman string-courses with heads on the south and west sides. The upper windows are interesting. They are double lights of Transitional character and divided by small columns. The arches are round on the east side and pointed elsewhere. On the north and east sides the original Transitional columns and mouldings remain : on the west their place has been taken in the 14th century by a mullion instead of a column and by scroll mouldings : on the south the old mouldings remain, but the column has been replaced in modern times by a thicker piece of masonry.

The parish register dates back to 1583.

At Corfton in this parish are the remains of a small chapel, now used as farm buildings. The position of two windows can be made out, but there is no interest about the building. There is no early reference to this chapel and I doubt whether it existed in mediæval times. Indeed tradition says that it was built in the last century for the convenience of an old gentleman living in the house near, who refused to go to the parish church less than a mile away. It appears to have been disused for something like a hundred years, but there is record of a marriage taking place there late in the 18th century. It is marked on the Ordnance Map as the Mount Chapel.

Easthope.

St. Peter.

HERE is record of this church as early as 1291, when it was valued at under £4 per annum, 3s. being paid to the Rector of Cound. The walls of the building may be as old as this or older, but there is no detail so ancient, unless it be the font, which is circular and very plain and rough, and may have been erected in very early times.

The east window is Decorated, having two lights with a quatrefoil in the head. In the south wall is a low side-window with the remains of a hinge: it is a broad cusped single light, such as might have been inserted in the 14th or 15th century. The window further west is a square-headed one with three mullions and a transom, all of wood: it is doubtless Elizabethan or somewhat later. The west window has two stone mullions and is also square-headed. On the north side is a small square-headed window, deeply splayed. The same wall has a small doorway, and a broad "bedroom" window low down. The gallery at the west end is lit by a "skylight."

It will be seen that there is very little *architectural* interest in the church. The most important thing to notice is the very quaint hour-glass, which is still attached to the pulpit. The actual glass is fitted into a wooden case, which rests in an iron frame, bearing the date 1662 (see Fig. 11).

Fig. 11.

I am doubtful whether the glass itself is original, but the stand and frame
certainly] are. The frame is four inches in height and six inches across.
Hour glasses had been in use in churches for some time before this one was
put up. An entry in the Ludlow churchwardens' accounts shews us that
one was made for that church in 1597 or 1598, the frame costing 1s. 8d.
They were probably not used before the reign of Elizabeth. They rarely
remain now in their original positions, and this one is therefore extremely
interesting.

Next to the hour-glass, the woodwork claims attention. The
trussed-rafter roof, ornamented over the chancel, and the wooden chancel arch
are said to be modern, but I think they must be partly ancient. The pulpit
is Jacobean, to which style belong two fine chairs within the communion
rails, and all the pews: those in the chancel are elaborately carved, but the
nave ones are plainer. On the south side of these there is the following
inscription

EDWARD : BALL. OF LONDON : GAVE THIS PULLPIT. AND
PEWES. TO. THIS PARISHE : WHEARE HE WAS BORNE : JUNE : 28 : ANNO
DOMINI : 1623 :

Opposite to this is the following

IT IS GOD. THAT WORKETH IN US. BOTH TO WILL : AND ALSO
TO WORKE : EVEN OF GOOD WILL : E. B. JUNE : 28 : ANNO DOMINI : 1623.

The south door and porch are of no special interest, except as
regards a few ancient tiles on the floor. Near the porch are some 18th
century tombs, bricked round in a curious manner. The walls are covered
with plaster, and also the small bell-turret at the west end. On the north
side, under a yew tree, are two ancient tombs with plain crosses.

The parish possesses a large flagon of date 1730, and other
comparatively modern plate. The register commences with the year 1624.

Halford.

Dedication unknown.

HALFORD is an ancient chapelry of Bromfield. It became a separate parish in 1841, and is held in conjunction with the living of Sibdon Carwood.

The church is finely situated on the left bank of the Onny, and is near the modern town of Craven Arms. It consists of chancel with vestry, nave, south porch, and double bell-gable at the west end. The nave is part of the original building, and dates from the Norman period. The south doorway is a semi-circular arch : the abaci are square, and the hood-moulding has rude leaves upon it, with a head in the centre of the arch. The only old window is the small lancet west of the door. The font may be Norman : it is very plain and circular and rests on a modern stem.

The old buttresses remain against the west wall, but they have been considerably restored. There is also a little of the old basement moulding,—a semi-hexagonal string-course, with a slope below.

The chapel was repaired in 1848, and in 1887 a considerable restoration took place. The chancel, vestry, and porch were built at this time, and also the roofs of nave and chancel, which are of the trussed-rafter form, that of the chancel being curved. All the modern work is excellent.

Heath.

Dedication unknown.

THIS is an ancient chapelry of the parish of Stoke St. Milborough. There is no MS. record of the church till a comparatively late period, but it nevertheless dates back to the 12th century, or the latter part of the 11th.

The church is very valuable for architectural study, as it is a wonderfully complete, though somewhat plain specimen of Norman work, with no admixture of other styles. It is a small building consisting of nave and chancel, the nave about half as long again as the chancel, and slightly wider. The chancel has one round-headed, deeply-splayed window in each of the three walls, and, underneath, a string-course of a common Norman form. There is a recess in the south wall, which may have been a piscina as well as an aumbry. The chancel arch is twice recessed and has the the usual hood and abaci, the capitals being scolloped.

The nave is very similar to the chancel. In the south wall there is one of the finely-splayed windows, and in the west another with two smaller ones above. The windows on the north side have been tampered with. One has been replaced by an oblong "bedroom" window, and the other has a stove chimney going through it. As in the chancel, a string-course is continued all the way round. The font is circular and slightly ornamented: it stands on two square plinths placed cross-wise. The pulpit and woodwork belong to the 17th century: the roof is a tie-beam one; that of the chancel is hidden by a plaster ceiling.

The exterior (see Plate XVI.) is even more thoroughly Norman than the interior. The only doorway of the church is on the south side. The zig-zag moulding of the arch is too shallow to be effective: the tympanum is plain. The capitals of the shafts have scolloping and small volutes: the plinths are square, without any proper bases. The door itself has some ancient ironwork: the hinges are of the crescent form, which was common in the 12th century. The buttresses are of the usual broad, thin character, and a string-course, like that inside the church, goes all the way round. The east and west windows are pierced right through buttresses. At the west end is a modern square opening for a bell, between two upper windows.

HEATH.

I hear that this ancient chapel is to be restored. There is certainly room for some repair, but it is to be earnestly hoped that nothing will be done to destroy the charming effect of this unusually complete and genuine example of the Norman style.

Holgate.

Holy Trinity.

HOLGATE church is a Saxon foundation, but the present building
dates from the Norman period. There is no Norman detail
in the eastern portion of the church, but this is not a sure
proof that that part, like the south and west walls of the nave
do not belong to this early period, particularly as there is no
sign in the masonry of any extension having taken place.
I suppose then that the chancel as well as the nave is Norman, and that the later windows were insertions of the Early
English and Decorated periods. The western tower was
evidently added in the 13th century, and the upper part built,
or rebuilt, in the Perpendicular period. The tower has been
recently repaired, and a restoration of the other parts of the
church has been begun, and is now (1894) going on.

THE INTERIOR.

In the east wall are two plain lancets, no doubt inserted in the
13th century. The north wall has a very good Decorated window of two
lights: the tracery in the head takes the characteristic form of the spherical
triangle, and the sill is ornamented with the scroll moulding so often seen
at this period. In the opposite wall is a three-light window in the same style,
but the design is not so good: there is a scoinson arch, but the tracery ends
with a square head. A broad lancet window west of the priest's doorway
may belong to the same period: the other window in the chancel is modern.
There is a plain pointed piscina, with a deep basin, in the south wall, and a
square aumbry underneath the Decorated window opposite. There are two
bold standards at the ends of a pew on the south side, and a 17th century
chair within the communion rails. A chancel arch has just been built and
the plaster taken off the roof: on the floor are several small brasses.

The nave contains some good woodwork. There are a number
of old oak pews with fillets worked upon them. It seems to me quite possible
that these may date back as far as the 14th century. Doors were added to
the pews in the 17th century, and one or two additional ones made. There
is some rich panelling of the same period against the north wall, with carvings
of leaves and grapes, and a coat of arms supposed to belong to a former

owner of the Coates Farm in the parish, but the name in not known. Against the south wall is placed an old misericord, which has some good carvings of griffins. Till this year there was a partition near the west end of the nave, which appears to have been built early in the present century, to allow that portion of the church to be used as a school : it recently served the purpose of a vestry. The only Norman window remaining is that in the west wall   it is deeply splayed, through the wall and a buttress of the usual Norman form ; it is now internal on account of the addition of the tower at the west end. The other windows of the nave are Decorated. On the south side is a good double light with a quatrefoil in the head : another window further east has no tracery, but the same moulding as this one,—the sunk chamfer on the jambs and scoinson arch. This reveals the Decorated style, and the two windows have doubtless been alike. In the north wall are two square-headed windows with the same characteristic moulding. The sunk chamfer also appears on a canopy in the south wall, and the roll and fillet as the hood-moulding : there is now no figure or sepulchral slab below. In the west wall is a rather large opening which needs explanation. There is no moulding or other detail to reveal its date, but it is almost of the shape of the spherical triangle, so often used in the 14th century. I do not feel satisfied that it is a hagioscope in this peculiar position, but I cannot say what else it could be. The doorway from the tower into the nave has a depressed arch, and can scarcely be of the same period as the tower itself. The roof of the nave has king-posts, and has recently parted with a considerable coating of plaster.

The two most elaborate features of this church are the font and the south doorway, both of Norman date. The font (see Fig. 12) is richly

Fig. 12.

carved, and remarkable. The upper moulding is the cable. Below is some
interlaced work, similar to that often seen on early crosses. The nail-head
ornament is also used and some grotesque representations of serpents. The
lower part of the bowl is carved with foliage of a late Norman type, and
below is a short stem with an upright zig-zag. The base has four curious
heads, and rests on a square block, which is placed on a much larger round
plinth.

The doorway (see Fig. 13) is of the same rich character and is

Fig. 13.

twice recessed. The hood-moulding has pellets on the eastern and diminutive
zig-zags on the western half. The next moulding is a large zig-zag, which
does not stand out very boldly, as a reference to the photograph will shew.
Next to this are rosettes, foliage, and other forms, and the inner moulding is
a row of rather poor beak-heads. All the shafts have ornamental capitals.
On the east side small volutes are the principal enrichments, combined with
foliage on two out of the three. Two of the western capitals also have foliage,

combined in one case with nail-heads: the outer capital is scolloped. The bases are slightly ornamented.

These two rich specimens are very interesting, as shewing the character of Norman carving in the latter part of the period. Grotesqueness is a marked feature of the ornament of the time and is shewn here in the curious animal forms on the font, and the beak-heads on the door. Classical influence is betrayed in the use of volutes and the cable moulding. Some of the foliage has quite a Byzantine appearance. The interlacing ornament is from Celtic sources, and the zig-zag, pellet, and cable were used by the Saxons before the Conquest.

THE EXTERIOR.

The porch on the south side has a wooden arch and barge-board, and may be as early as the 14th century: the roof displays bold double braces between the purlins. The buttresses against the south wall of the nave have the bell-shaped base-moulding used from the middle of the 14th century onwards: they are probably Decorated, as the projection is almost equal to the breadth. There is a curious carving of the upper part of a human figure in the south chancel wall.

The buttresses on the north side have not the base-moulding just mentioned: they do not project quite so far as the southern ones, and may be of the 13th century.

The tower is 22 ft. 6 in. broad, and about 1 ft. wider than the nave. The lower part is Early English, the basement-moulding being of the common form of a heavy roll with a slope below, similar to that shewn in Fig. 14, A. There are two characteristic buttresses of greater breadth than projection. The early windows which remain are narrow and square-headed: some others have been blocked. All the upper part of the tower is Perpendicular, and was built, or rebuilt, in the 15th century. The four windows are all different: that on the east is square-headed, the one on the south is pointed, that on the west is pointed within a square moulding, and the northern window is in the form of the shouldered arch, not generally used at such a late period. Two string-courses are used, and a good battlement with four pinnacles, ornamented with stars and other designs. The pitch of a former nave roof can be seen against the tower.

There are remains of an ancient cross in the churchyard. The parish register commences with the year 1661.

Hope Bowdler.

St. Andrew.

THIS church is modern, but the parish is an ancient one and there is a reference to the church in the year 1291. A sketch made by the Rev. J. Brooke in 1859 shews that the old church consisted of nave, chancel, south porch, and western tower. The windows were small, and the tower had a pyramidal roof. The church may therefore have dated from Norman times, but the present building, which was erected in 1863, is a copy, more or less, of the Early English style. It has the same parts as the old church had, and an apsidal vestry on the south side. There is some good modern glass in one of the north chancel windows. The pulpit is well carved and bears the date 1639 : there is a also a chest of about the same period.

The parish possesses a chalice of the year 1572.

The registers begin early in 1564, but are fragmentary between 1752 and 1780, and altogether missing between 1780 and 1784, so far as the general register of baptisms and burials is concerned.

Hopton Cangeford.

Dedication unknown.

THIS was formerly a chapelry of the parish of Staunton Lacey, and there is record of an incumbent as early as 1325. A separate parish, for a very small population, appears to have been formed, and a church built, in the early part of the 18th century. A tombstone in the churchyard has the date 1745, and a monument in the church records a death in 1731. The church cannot be much earlier than this, for it is quite Georgian in style. It is built chiefly of brick, and consists of a small polygonal chancel, nave, and western tower. There is a gallery at the west end. The font is modern.

The register dates from 1816.

Ludlow.

St. John.

HIS church was erected in 1881 at the cost of the late Hon. Mary
Windsor-Clive, and from the designs of Sir Arthur Blomfield.
It consists of chancel, nave, south aisle, south porch, and
western bell gable. The north wall has an arcade inserted in
it to provide for a future addition of a north aisle. The
general style of the church is late Early English, with lancet
and plate tracery windows.

St. Leonard.

HIS is a small church, erected by Sir Gilbert Scott in 1870.
The design is Early English, lancet windows being used, and
the building consists of chancel, nave, bell-gable at the intersection, and south porch.

It stands near the site of an ancient chapel
dedicated to St. Leonard, which was pulled down in the last
century.

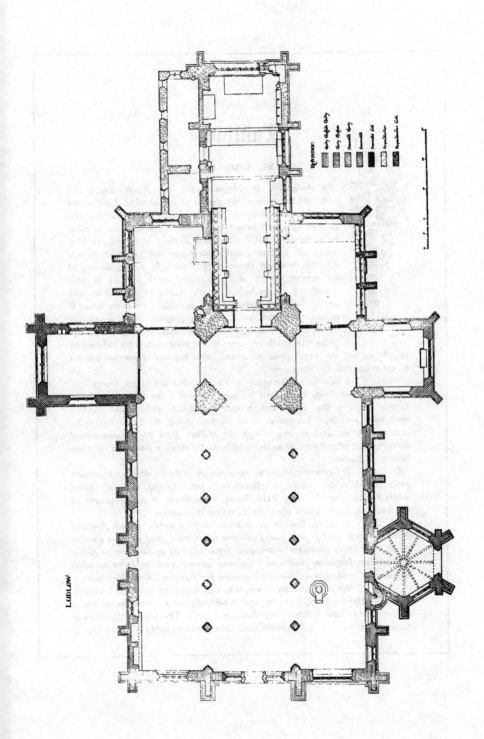

Ludlow.

St. Lawrence.

IN the *Antiquities of Shropshire* the Rev. R. W. Eyton has expressed the opinion that the church or chapel of Ludlow was originally dependent on Bromfield, and that it was founded at least 150 years before Domesday. The evidence of coins seems to shew that Ludlow was a place of importance long before the Conquest, and it no doubt had its parish church. All this, however, throws very little light on the history of the present church of St. Lawrence, which belongs to later periods. It is the largest parish church in Shropshire, and one of the most interesting and beautiful. Its noble tower is of unusual height, and its internal proportions are grand and impressive. The hexagonal porch is almost unique; the carvings of the misericords are some of the most remarkable to be found anywhere; and the church possesses several other features of peculiar interest to the artist and the antiquary.

I have found the study which this church requires a very considerable undertaking, but I shall be amply repaid if the following account throws light on the many architectural difficulties which exist in this remarkable building. I must as usual confine myself chiefly to the architecture, and not deal at length with the stained glass, the churchwardens' accounts, and other historical matter which should obtain a place in a complete history of Ludlow.

Before commencing an examination of the building, an important piece of MS. evidence must be referred to. John Leland, the well-known writer of the time of Henry VIII., found a document at the monastery of Cleobury Mortimer, which gives the following information:

Anno D. 1199, contigit in quadam Angliae patria, scilicet provincia Salopesbiriensi, apud pagum quae Ludelavia nuncupatur, quod pagenses ejusdem oppidi decrevissent ecclesiam suam, quod brevis esset ad continendam se plebem contingentem, longiorem construere. Quocirca oportuit quendam terrae tumulum magnum ad occidentem ecclesiae solo coaequare, qua murus ejusdem debuit extendi.

We must give some weight to this document, but should, I think, be careful about trusting it too far, as it is evidently not a contemporary record and may have been written long after the event. The words "decrevissent ecclesiam suam . . . longiorem construere" seem to imply that they merely *extended* an existing church in 1199, and, as the next sentence shews us, at the west end. We may fairly treat the document as good evidence to prove that considerable alterations were made to Ludlow church in 1199, but I do not think we need consider it an accurate description of exactly what was done.

Is there then evidence in the present building of work being carried out about this period? There certainly is, and I think we shall see that the alterations consisted of a remodelling, if not an entire rebuilding of the church.

In dealing with the history of the main features of the building I must depart from my usual custom, and place side by side the conclusions at which I have arrived, and the evidence which supports them; and not first state the conclusions and leave the proofs to be gathered amidst the necessarily lengthy descriptions of the church.

What evidence then is there of architectural work of about the year 1199? It will be observed that the plinth moulding shewn in Fig. 14,A,

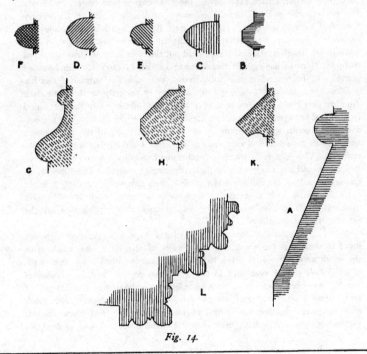

Fig. 14.

goes round the outside of most of the building. At first sight one might suppose that this indicated the same period throughout, but the problem is not so easy: the same moulding appears, copied by later builders, on the walls of the north aisle and the transepts. More certain evidence is supplied by the flat, slightly projecting buttresses which remain, and round which this plinth moulding is carried. There is one against the south wall of the lady chapel, one against the south wall of the nave near the porch, and the remains of four buttresses of like character and similar projection against the west wall of the nave and the south-west corner of the south aisle (see Plan). These buttresses are quite of Norman character: the projection of Early English and later buttresses is never so slight. However, the moulding already referred to is of Early English form, though it does occur in late Norman work. We therefore come to the conclusion that this moulding, combined with the slightly projecting buttresses, must probably be referred to the Transition period. Indeed, the combination may be seen on the buttresses at the west end of Buildwas Abbey, which may be dated circa 1170. Now, the great change from Norman to Early English may be said to have been more or less effected at Canterbury Cathedral between 1174 and 1184, but pure Early English work, without admixture of Norman, was perhaps not built till between 1192 and 1200—the work of St. Hugh at Lincoln. We need not therefore be in the least surprised to find a Norman feeling still remaining at Ludlow in 1199. A round-headed piscina will be noticed in the lady chapel, near the flat buttress: this has a fillet upon the arch (see Fig. 19), and fits in perfectly to the same date. Another detail which points to a very early part of the Early English period is the semi-hexagonal string-course (see Fig. 14,B), which is found on the outside of the south wall of the nave; inside the south wall of the lady chapel; and outside the south and east walls of the same building, but almost entirely renewed. This is a form which is much more common in Norman times than any other, and but rarely seen in the Early English period. The same string-course is used on the outside walls of St. John's chapel, and, though it is not there combined with other strong indications of early work, it is I think sufficient to shew that this building was erected at the same time as the other parts just mentioned.

To sum up then, we have what I hope will appear quite enough proof to shew that the south and west walls of the nave and south aisle, the south and east walls of the lady chapel, and the north and east walls of St. John's chapel were built in the Transition period; and, on account of the MS. evidence, these parts may be referred to about the year 1199. It follows that this Transitional church consisted of *at least* nave and south aisle; chancel extending as far east as the chapels do; and these chapels themselves, which may have been merely chancel aisles. I say *at least*, for

there may have been a central tower: there certainly was one previous to
that now standing, as will be shewn presently. I can find no proof of a
north aisle to the building of this period, though of course there may have
been one. Whether the builders of 1199 made a clean sweep of the church
which previously existed or not we cannot tell, but I have been unable to
discover anything in the present building which belongs indisputably to the
pure Norman period or earlier. It is perhaps open to anyone to maintain
that all these early parts were built a little before 1199, with the combination
of the flat buttresses and the mouldings shewn in Fig 14,A and B; but, if
so, I do not see how we can give any weight to the documentary evidence
that, at any rate, the *western* part of the church was built in 1199. For this
western part has the same mouldings as the lady chapel, and I think was
evidently built at the same time. The round-headed piscina, with its fillet,
might perhaps have been an insertion, but it seems to be part of the original
work, and the use of the fillet precludes the idea that it can have been erected
earlier than the Transition period.

I believe then that a careful examination of the church will
convince anyone that the work of 1199 was a rebuilding, and not a mere
enlargement, and that the parts of this church which I have mentioned still
remain.

Some years after this great alteration, and in the pure Early
English period, the south doorway of the church was inserted, and windows
in the south aisle, the jambs of which still remain. The trefoil-headed piscina
in the lady chapel, and the little window in the east wall of the chancel, to
be referred to presently, also belong to this style. But I think there was a
more important addition at the time, namely, an extension of the chancel
by two bays. To prove that these were built later than the lady chapel, it
is only necessary to examine the north-east corner of that building outside,
at the point where it joins the south wall of the chancel. It is true that
the same plinth moulding (Fig. 14,A) is used on both walls, but it has
already been shewn that this is no sure indication that they belong to the
same date. The important point to notice is that the stones of this basement
moulding *are not bonded at the corner.* I have carefully examined every other
example in the church where this moulding goes round a corner at the same
level, and *in every instance* the stones are bonded, and indicate that the parts
in question were built at the same time. At first sight the heavy roll
moulding at this corner appears to be bonded, but a little care will reveal
the joint. This is still more apparent in the stones which compose the slope.
One wall has more of these than the other, and they are not bonded, but
those of the lady chapel wall are continued right past those of the chancel
wall, and it is quite clear that the lady chapel must have been built first.

The plinth moulding is continued to the end of the farthest bay but one of the chancel, and there stops abruptly (see Plan). This south wall has, on the whole, a Perpendicular appearance, but that does not shew that the lower part is not earlier: I am only now concerned to prove that this wall is later than that of the lady chapel. It has already been pointed out that the first bay of the chancel is of the same date as the chapels, but the walls of the second and third bays are of a different thickness from that of the first, a fact which in itself makes a difference of date probable. It will have been noticed that in this south wall we have clear proof of a later date than 1199, but none to shew at what subsequent time it was erected before the Perpendicular period. The missing evidence is supplied in the north wall, which, it is reasonable to suppose, was erected at the same time. On the north side of this wall, as can be observed by going into the western division of the vestry, is a string-course, covered with whitewash, of the form generally called the pear or keel moulding (see Fig. 14,C). Above, is a remnant of a window-jamb, which exactly corresponds with the outer moulding of the inner jambs, which formed part of the Early English windows in the south aisle. The pear moulding is used in the Decorated period, but is more common in the Early English. This evidence then, combined with that of the window-jamb, makes it probable that this wall, and, in consequence, the second and third bays of the chancel were added in the Early English period. It is true that both these details *might* be Decorated, but they are more commonly Early English, and I shall presently bring forward further evidence from the vestry to shew that the 13th century is a more probable period than the 14th for the addition of these two bays to the chancel.

We now come to the Decorated period, when a considerable portion of the present building was erected. The work of this time apparently commenced with the porch, the windows of which are early Decorated. Next came the north aisle, which may have replaced an earlier building on the same site, but which in its present form belongs almost entirely to the early part of the 14th century. The south transept was evidently erected about the middle of the Decorated period, some of the windows having the reticulated tracery often used at that time: the evidence outside agrees with this so far as it goes. The north transept was built near the end of the Decorated period, probably circa 1370: the window tracery is of a later type than that in the south transept, but not of the developed Perpendicular. Of course there may have been transepts in the Transitional church, but there is no evidence of their existence. Certain other alterations, which will be mentioned presently, were also effected in the 14th century.

A great transformation took place in the 15th century, and it will be noticed that the general appearance of the interior of the church is

Perpendicular.   It is difficult to say whether the chancel or nave was first dealt with.   In the former, large arches were inserted to divide the chapels from the first bay of the chancel: whether there were arches or plain walls before, we cannot say.   The two Early English bays were partly rebuilt and one bay added at the east end.   It is true that there is a small Early English window in the east wall, but the wall is so thoroughly Perpendicular below this, as well as above, that it must have been moved from elsewhere.   Further evidence will be mentioned later on to prove that the eastern bay was an addition.   The present vestry seems to have been erected at the same time that the alterations to the chancel took place.   The nave arcades were entirely rebuilt in this period, and, as will presently be proved, the tower was rebuilt shortly after the nave.

The same masons' marks have been found on all this Perpendicular work, and therefore it was probably all accomplished in one generation. It will be shewn further on that the chancel was altered in the middle of the 15th century or earlier, and that the tower was nearly finished in 1470.   If then we suppose that the chancel was altered *first*, as the tower certainly was *last*, we get a period of *at least* 20 years for the whole of the Perpendicular work.   Of course it may have been more, and probably was, but the same masons' marks being used seems to shew that it cannot have been a long period.

Such I believe to be an outline of the history of St. Lawrence's church, Ludlow.   At the risk of repeating myself further on, I have considered it advisable to deal at some length with the evidence which supports many of the statements I have made.   However, the account would have lost in clearness if I had detailed all the minor changes of which we have proofs. So far, only the most important alterations and additions have been mentioned ; the others will now be referred to in the course of a necessarily lengthy description of the church.

Before proceeding, I must refer briefly to the various restorations that the building has recently undergone.   In 1859-1860 very considerable alterations were made by Sir Gilbert Scott.   The porch, which was in a very ruinous condition, was repaired ; and the tracery of many of the windows renewed.   The old pews and galleries were swept away, the stained glass partly "restored," and a host of other changes made.   A full account of the restoration will be found in a book on the church by Mr. J. T. Irvine, who was clerk of the works at the time.   More recently, in 1889-1891, the tower and lady chapel have been recased by Sir Arthur Blomfield.

A wonderful picture of the state of the church from the Reformation period onwards is obtained by a study of the churchwardens' accounts.   Some few remain for a year or two previous to 1471, but there is then a break

PLATE ~~XVIII~~ XVII.

LUDLOW.
THE CHANCEL.

till 1540, after which they are continuous. The accounts from 1540 to 1574 were transcribed in 1869 by the late Mr. Thomas Wright, F.S.A. for the Camden Society, and all the others are being transcribed by Mr. Llewellyn Jones for the Transactions of the Shropshire Archaeological Society : the publication has now been brought as far as 1749. After perusing these accounts the strongest impression left on the mind is perhaps that they tell us of a state of things in the church very different from the present. It *may* have been advisable to clear away the old pews and galleries, to remove the tombstones, and so on, but it is certain that by this means a page in the history of the church has been almost entirely blotted out. If one or two debased pinnacles and buttresses are removed, there will be nothing in the church to shew a future generation that there ever was an 18th century.

A reference to the Plan will shew that the church now consists of chancel of four bays, with double vestry on the north side ; chapels on either side of the first bay of the chancel ; central tower ; north and south transepts ; nave and aisles of six bays ; and south porch. Besides the chapels referred to, St. John's and the lady chapel, the churchwardens' accounts speak of those of St. Catherine, St. Margaret, St. Steven, and the Trinity ; also of " Allhallon chaunselle," " Beawpie chapelle," " the butchers chancell," Cooke's chapel, " the rode chauncelle," " the showmakers Chauncell," " the skolars chancell," " the weavers chauncell," " the wen' chauncelle," and " Wyattes chancelle" : it is implied that there was a chapel of St. George. There is also evidence of a chapel of St. Edmund the King, the fletchers' chapel, and the Warwick chapel. It is a little difficult to see how this astonishing number of chapels could be contained in the building, but all their names do not necessarily mean different parts of the church. For example, the butchers', scholars' and weavers' chapels are no doubt the same as some of those dedicated to various saints. It is now impossible to fix the position of all these chapels, but there is some evidence as to the parts occupied by those of St. Catherine, St. Edmund, St. Margaret, St. Steven, and Beawpie chapel, the fletchers' chapel, the scholars' chapel, the Warwick chapel, and the wedding chapel. This will be dealt with when describing the different parts of the building referred to.

THE CHANCEL

is constantly referred to in the churchwardens' accounts as the high chancel. It belongs, as I have already stated, to three periods. The first bay is a long one, and was built about 1199 : the second and third bays were added in the 13th century, and the eastern bay in the 15th. To the same period belong the large arches in the first bay, and the appearance of the chancel is almost entirely Perpendicular. Indeed a considerable portion of the older walls was rebuilt in the 15th century. A large reddish ashlar was used, quite different from the small white stone which appears over the arches of the first bay. Small stones can also be seen low down on the north side, under the third window from the east end, and they are still more evident on the other side of this same wall: the same feature appears low down in the south wall, at the east end of the stalls. There are also some details of 13th century date. The jambs and arch of the east window are composed of Early English moulded stones, and some fragments of the same period may be observed *outside* the small windows over the first bay on the north side. All the windows themselves are Perpendicular of good design, the east window of nine lights being particularly fine (see Plate XVII.). The stained glass in this window represents the legend of the patron saint, St. Lawrence, who was broiled to death on a gridiron at Rome in the third century. Portions o. the glass are original, and the remainder was "restored" in 1828—1832 by Mr. David Evans of Shrewsbury. One of the figures in the window is a bishop, before whom is the inscription

THOMAS SPOFORD DEI GRATIA HEREFORD. EPUS.

This seems to imply that the window was erected in the time of Spoford, who was bishop of Hereford from 1422 to 1448. It may perhaps be maintained that it is a memorial window to the bishop, but I think it is fair to infer that it would be erected in, or very near his time, and this evidence therefore shews us that the great alterations to the chancel, including the rebuilding of the east wall, took place *at least* as early as the middle of the 15th century.

There is stained glass in the three large windows on the north and south sides. This has been considerably restored.

The reredos at first sight appears to be entirely modern, but some of the smaller figures are original. The foliage certainly looks like Decorated work, and, if it is so, the reredos must have been erected in the 14th century, and moved when the chancel was extended in the Perpendicular period. All the large figures are modern, the restoration being under the direction of Mr. R. Kyrke Penson, F.S.A. Some fragments of the old work are preserved in the Ludlow Museum.

It has been generally supposed that the reredos was mutilated in the time of Cromwell, but this is a mistake. In the churchwardens' accounts for 1548, 6s. 8d. was paid "for takynge downe of the roode and the images." This cannot refer to images in the rood loft, for we have in the same year, "for nayles to hange up clothes when the images was pullede downe . . . iiijd." No curtains would have been required where images had been in the rood loft. Again, in 1559—60, we have "Paid for lyme to washe and plaster the walle where the auctor stode in the hie chaunselle . . . iiijd." Cromwell is therefore innocent of the mutilation of the reredos, as he no doubt is of a number of other things which have been put down to his destructive hand.

This is not the place to enter into a long discussion of the original purpose of what are called low side-windows, but I must call attention to the very remarkable position of a small opening of that class in the east wall. It has already been shewn that, though Early English, it is now in a Perpendicular wall (see Fig. 15). It was no doubt moved from the south

Fig. 15.

wall, when the alterations took place in the 15th century : I am not aware of any other instance of a low side-window in the east wall. A careful examination of it may throw some light on this much discussed question. It will be observed that the window is near the outside face of the wall, and does not appear from the chancel (see Plan and Fig. 16). The wall is here very thick, about 4ft. 6in., and a small chamber is formed in the thickness of the wall. This is entered by a door in the south wall, and the chamber quickly turns to the left, and a stone erection nearly 3ft. from the floor (CB) has to be mounted before the window is reached. The whole space from CB to ED is of this level, and the part beyond ED is slightly lower. There is no shutter by the window, but there has evidently been one across CB, the hinges still remaining. There is another door in the reredos, which must have had some object : it is absolutely useless for access to the chamber, for, in order to support the upper part of the heavy wall, there is a mass of masonry which would completely prevent the smallest man from getting through the door. What then was it for? If it were necessary to disprove the popular idea that these windows were "leper windows" this example would be quite sufficient. No one outside the window could possibly have seen the elevation of the

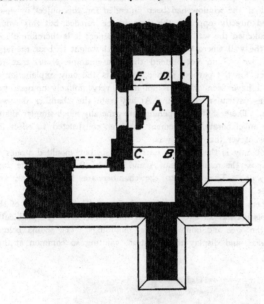

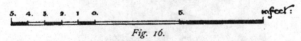

Fig. 16.

host. Nor can the window have been used for the priest to hand the consecrated elements through. It is not likely that he would have had to climb to such a height to do it, and if so he would have entered by the door in the south wall, and that in the reredos would have been useless. Is it not most likely that the door in the reredos was made to allow a person in the chamber to see something going on in the chancel? The Rev. Dr. Cox, F.S.A., has given close attention to the subject of low side-windows, and is "convinced that the one theory which reasonably accounts for the great majority of them, and which has documentary evidence on its side, is that they were used for the purpose of ringing the sanctus bell therefrom at the time of Mass." Now if anyone will seat himself on the stone erection in this chamber (at A) he will observe that it would have been possible for him to see the elevation of the host in the chancel, and, at the same time, to ring a bell through the window. It may be objected that if the window had been intended for this object it would have been placed directly opposite the door in the reredos, but this would perhaps have weakened the wall too much at the corner; it is therefore placed in that part of the wall where there is not so much weight to bear, the large window being above. I do not pretend that this example *proves* that the window was used for the purpose named, but it is the only explanation of these windows I have seen, which is not made very unlikely or destroyed altogether by this particular example. At any rate the chamber deserves careful attention. These shuttered openings are generally much simpler affairs, but in this case an elaborate arrangement has been constructed to effect the desired object, whatever that object was.

Not only is the window Early English, but moulded stones of that period compose the masonry near A and part of the wall by the door in the south wall. The doors to the chamber are Perpendicular, and have ogee arches.

There are four sedilia and a piscina in the south wall of the chancel. The piscina has an ogee arch, and the characteristic Perpendicular combination of the ogee and hollow chamfer mouldings. The sedilia belong to the same period, and display the imitation vaulting so common at that time.

Fig. 17.

The Easter sepulchre in the north wall is considerably shorn of its original splendour: it is crocketed, and partly panelled with quatrefoils; the cusps terminate in an ornamental manner. Underneath the arch is now a rich tomb of very beautiful design (see Fig. 17). We learn by an inscription that it commemorates Sir Robert Towneshend, Chief Justice of the Marches of Wales and Chester, his wife Alice, and six sons and six daughters. All of these are represented on the tomb. Small figures of the daughters are at each end, and of the sons along the front. The knight is represented in armour of the Elizabethan character, with ruffs, and his feet rest against a stag. Dame Alice wears the Mary Queen of Scots cap, and the costume of the period: her feet rest against three dogs. The tomb is Elizabethan, and an interesting example of the style of ornamentation in vogue at the time. The design is on the whole Classical, with Ionic columns; but there is a little Gothic feeling remaining, as is shewn by the panelling of the miniature buttresses, and by the same feature under a semi-circular arch at the east end. Sir Robert's crest is represented above the centre of the older arch, and along the entablature below is the inscription

MEMENTO MORI RESPICE FINEM.

A tombstone has been placed against the wall under the arch, with poor imitations of the cusps on the panelling near.

The same plan of accommodating older ornament can be seen under the second window on the south side. The tomb is Classical, but the Gothic panelling of the wall under the window is made to do duty to adorn it. The tomb is that of the wife and fourth daughter of Sir Henry Sydney, Lord President of the Council of Wales: the former died at Ludlow Castle in 1574.

The large alabaster monument further west has Doric and Corinthian columns, and no trace of Gothic design. It is dated 1592, and commemorates Edmund Walter, Chief Justice of three Shires in South Wales, and Mary his wife. The figures wear Elizabethan costume with ruffs, and the male has no armour. The railings round this tomb are original, as also are the two graceful iron standards, with the initials of the persons here represented (see Plate XVII.).

On the opposite side are two later tombs of Classical design. One has two kneeling figures, representing Edward Waties, Esquire, and his wife, Martha: she died in 1629, and the monument was erected before her husband's death. The other has a figure of a cherub, and commemorates Theophilus Salwey, Esquire, who died in 1760.

The panelling below the large Perpendicular windows has already been referred to. It is not precisely the same on all the bays, but each division has a cinquefoiled arch. At the base of the panelling runs a stone ledge, which forms a natural and convenient finish to it.

The present level of the chancel is probably the old one, for the position of the doors, the sedilia, and other original features, indicates that it cannot have been materially altered. The mosaic pavement within the communion rails has lately been added, from the design of Sir Arthur Blomfield.

The roof is a very fine one, though rather flat. The corbels have representations of angels, and there are also angels in the centre of the tie-beams holding shields, on which are carved ascriptions of praise. The colouring on the roof is modern, but some traces of the original colour were discovered when the church was restored.

One of the most beautiful features of St. Lawrence's church is the rich stall work, which fortunately retains a good deal of its original carving. This reminds us that the church was collegiate. Leland says, "This Church has been much advanced by a Brotherhood therein founded in the name of St. John the Evangelist, the original whereof was (as the people say there) in the time of Edward the Confessor, and it is constantly affirmed there, that the pilgrims that brought the ring from St. John the Evangelist to King Edward were the inhabitants of Ludlow." Leland also tells us that there was here a college of ten priests, connected with St. John's chapel, and also connected, we may suppose, with the larger brotherhood. There are still remains of this college, at the north west of the church.

This brotherhood of pilgrims or palmers was evidently an important one at Ludlow at an early period. We cannot be sure that it dates back to the time of Edward the Confessor, but we know that it received a royal charter of incorporation in the year 1283 as the "Palmers' Guild." It was certainly in a flourishing state during the 15th century, but in the 16th it was dissolved and its property granted to the town of Ludlow by Edward VI.

It is a matter of conjecture how much of the extensive alterations of the 15th century we owe to the guild, and how much to the parish. All doubt however with regard to the stalls is removed by a record which tells us that 100 planks to make new stalls were bought at Bristol in 1447 *with the money of the guild.*

The original canopies, with the exception of some at the west end, have disappeared; those on the north and south sides are modern and the crest above them. The cornice is beautifully carved with grapes and leaves. There are sixteen stalls on each side, and between them are cherubs, some holding shields. There are six standards on each side, which are carved in the most exquisite manner with foliage and figures: the time and care spent on them are truly wonderful. Four of those on the north side have had figures, but they have disappeared and only the recesses remain. The

same remark applies to the first and fourth on the south side, counting
from the east. One of the figures on the second is that of a bishop with a
mitre. The fifth has the Good Shepherd on the east side, St. Peter on the
west, and cherubs on the north and south. On the south side of the sixth
is apparently a carving of the Virgin and dead Christ. Some of the figures
have been mutilated and are difficult to make out. The same may be said
of several of the misericords, but many of them are nearly perfect, and they
constitute one of the finest series of this class of carving to be seen
anywhere. It is difficult to be certain whether all of them belong to this
period or not: some may have been part of the old stalls which preceded
the present ones. Nos. 3, 5, 7, counting from the east, on the north side,
and Nos. 1, 8, 9, 12, 13 on the south seem to be the work of one artist,
each of these having a carving of a small spray of leaves at the side. The
following is a description :—

NORTH SIDE.

(1.) Two boys, one with a mirror, making fun of a smirking woman,
apparently because she wears the horned head-dress (see Fig.
18). This would seem to point to an earlier date than 1447,
for the horned head-dress came into fashion in the reign of
Henry V., but it may have been sufficiently new at Ludlow
in this year to excite the derision of street boys.

(2.) Another caricature of the horned head-dress, which is worn by
a winged animal. Griffins on either side.

(3.) This has the spray and is one of the most striking. The device
of giving short weights and measures is not confined to any
age, and we have here an offending mediæval ale-wife, carried
by a demon ; and her soul, represented by a naked body,
thrust into hell by another. One demon plays the pipes, and
another reads from a scroll the sins of the unfortunate
woman.

(4.) A mermaid holding a mirror. Fishes with large heads at the
sides.

(5.) By the same carver as No. 3 : it has been mutilated. One
figure is on the ground, and another is being pushed towards
him by a third. On one side is a pot on the fire, and on
the other a leaf.

(6.) A chained animal. At the sides, heads with leaves in the
mouth.

(7.) A mitred hishop. Mitres at the sides : these are lower than
was usual in the middle of the 15th century, and they may
be earlier. The spray is again carved.

(8.)   Prince of Wales' feathers.

(9.)   A fox with mitre and cope preaching to geese, not unlike one
of the misericords at Ripon. The mitre is higher than those
in No. 7, and of the ordinary Perpendicular character. On
one side is a leaf, and on the other two human figures, one
with the hand raised, and a small animal below.

(10.) A stag. A dog on either side.

(11.) A crowned figure. Leaf at each side.

(12.) An angel. Leaf at each side.

(13.) A hawk and lures.

(14.) Plain.

(15.) Leaves and Tudor roses.

(16.) Plain.

Fig. 18.

SOUTH SIDE.

(1.)   This has the spray. In the middle is a figure with three pairs
of bellows, a barrel and hammer. On the right is a figure
sitting, and on the left a panelled tomb with pick, spades, etc.,
and a hand holding a pot. I can give no satisfactory
explanation of this.

(2.)   Leaves.

(3.)   A smirking figure, with pack on back, pulling on long boots.
Leaf at each side.

(4.) Horned head-dress on either side and the older form in the middle.

(5.) An owl. Another bird at each side.

(6.) A goose. Leaf at each side.

(7.) A hooded figure sitting and warming hands and feet at a fire. On one side a pot on the fire, and on the other two pieces of meat hanging up.

(8.) This has the spray and is difficult to decipher. On one side is a horse, and on the other a money bag and a cushion. In the middle are five figures. One is standing, and the others are struggling in pairs. The scene may perhaps represent an encounter with robbers or a fight about the price of the horse (see Fig. 18).

(9.) By the same carver again. Various mutilated birds and animals. Leaf at each side.

(10.) A large winged animal. Head of bird at each side.

(11.) A figure holding a jug to a barrel. Leaf at each side.

(12.) The spray again. At the sides barrels, cups, and jugs. In the centre a large cask with a kneeling figure on either side. This is apparently a glorification of the ale cask, really or ironically, the figures acting as supporters to the coat of arms of a barrel.

(13.) By the same workman. A seated figure holding a scroll. Face at each side.

(14.) Plain.

(15.) A Tudor rose with a large ring on one side.

(16.) Plain.

On the whole it would appear as if the eight carvings with the spray, and perhaps two or three of the others, were done some time before 1447, but I suppose that most of the misericords must be put down to this date and also the whole of the stalls. Below these on each side is a row of pierced quatrefoils, some of which are original.

The screen at the west end of the chancel is a beautiful piece of work. It is of considerable depth and coved on the west side to support the rood loft. Underneath this is imitation vaulting with some finely carved bosses. The organ stood here till 1860, and was approached by a staircase inside the screen on the south side. The approach, at an earlier period, to the rood loft must have been here also, as the wooden four-centred arch, now blocked, is original and must have been a doorway. The rood has of course disappeared. It has been stated above that it was taken down in 1548, and in the same year we are told that sixpence was paid "to William

Marteyne for a dayes worke makynge the rode loft playne." In 1554, after the accession of Mary, we have, " paid for the settynge up of the rood . . iiijd." Finally in 1559 there is an entry, " for takynge downe the rowde . . . . . vjd." It seems strange that it should have cost more to take it down than to put it up.

The accounts speak of the rood chancel. This would I suppose be a small chapel with an altar against the screen. We know that altars were sometimes placed in the rood loft, but this was probably not the case here, for we read in 1548 of a pew by the "rode chauncelle."

THE VESTRY,

as has already been stated, was built about the same time as the Perpendicular additions to the chancel. In the north wall are three windows and a doorway, but this doorway was a window at one time. The form of it exactly corresponds with the windows, and the stones where the moulding ceases were cut into, when the transformation took place. Mediaeval vestries rarely had entrances from the outside, and all doubt with regard to this one is set at rest by several entries in the churchwardens' accounts for the year 1569. The sums of money given to the various workmen who made the transformation are detailed with great exactitude. This doorway therefore is no proof that the present level of the vestry is the original one, and the piscina low down in the east wall might be thought to shew that the level had been raised. However, piscinae were sometimes placed low down in a vestry, and nothing definite can be gathered from the position of this one. I discuss this matter of the floor level on account of a very remarkable feature in the western division of the building, generally called "the dark vestry." This is a recess in the south wall, *i.e.* the north wall of the chancel, about 3 ft. wide, 1 ft. deep, and having its top 9 in. from the floor (see Plan). This cannot have been part of a doorway, or else, after disuse, it would have been filled up in a very different manner from this. The top is composed of a sepulchral slab with a cross incised upon it, and the whole thing certainly has the appearance of a fireplace : the flue still goes up about 4 ft. The remarkable point is that it is far too low to have been used as such at the present level of the floor. An easy way out of the difficulty is to suppose that it was made as a fireplace to this Perpendicular building, and that the floor has since been raised ; but there is other evidence to be taken into account. Against the west wall is a very distinct mark of the pitch of a roof, lower than the present roof. This cuts into a semi-hexagonal string-course, for it must be remembered that the wall is the east wall of St. John's chapel and Transitional in date. It is most important to notice that this former roof could not have been used for the present vestry. It would have been almost if not quite too low for the most westerly window; it would have cut right into the other north windows, and still more so into the east window. There is, therefore, clear proof that there was a building on this site before the Perpendicular vestry was erected. The north wall of this building was probably on the same site as the present one, as the mark of the roof stops there: we cannot say how far it extended eastwards. There is no necessity then to suppose that the level of the floor has been altered since Perpendicular times, or that the fireplace has ever been used for the present vestry: there is not the slightest sign of an exit for the smoke in the wall above the roof; the Perpendicular string-course runs on uninterruptedly. It seems clear then that the fireplace was used for the earlier building, which I have proved to have existed. It is an interesting problem to try and find out at what period this was erected. It must have been after the addition of the two Early English bays to the chancel, for the string course (Fig. 14, C) and the window jamb above, already referred to, shew that this was an external wall at that time. The form of the cross which composes the mantel does not help us much: it may date from the 12th century. However, it is clear that the building was erected *after* the Early English bays of the chancel, and *before* the Perpendicular vestry. The flue would come very close to the old window jamb, but might easily avoid it. We cannot then be far wrong in supposing the erection of this building to have taken place late in the 13th century or in the 14th. These considerations supply us with the further proof I spoke of early in the account that the addition of the two bays to the chancel took place in the Early English period rather than in the Decorated. We can hardly suppose that a building would have been erected here and taken down between a 14th century addition to the chancel and a 15th century building of a vestry. As I mentioned before, the pear or keel moulding, which composes the string course (see Fig. 14, C), is a possible Decorated form, but if it had been Decorated in this case we should expect to have seen it again in the other Decorated work in the church, of which we have at least three periods, but we do not: D, E, and F in Fig. 14 are used but not C.

All this evidence is I think convincing that the two bays were added to the chancel in the 13th century, and a building erected on the north side of it in the 14th. Whether this building was a vestry or not I am not prepared to say: it is certainly unusual to find a fireplace in such an early part of a parish church.

East of the old window jamb is a corbel, which evidently supported the roof of the earlier building: indeed there are still remains of the beams at the ends. The fact of the east end remaining, surrounded by Perpendicular masonry, almost seems to show that the 15th century builders intended at first to retain the old roof, and made a new one at a higher level as an after-thought.

There is an old chest here with four locks.

A reference to the Plan will show that the partition between the two vestries corresponds to a buttress on the south side: it is pierced with a good pointed arch, and the door is an ancient one. Above this arch, on the east side, is a recess, the use of which is not apparent : there is another in the buttress farther east.

The doorway to the vestry from the chancel is more depressed than we might expect before the middle of the 15th century, but it should be remembered that the form of an arch was very often dictated merely by convenience and this low form fits in best with the window above. The doorway is panelled in a similar way to the walls on either side, though the divisions are smaller. I see no reason to doubt that the door itself, with its panelling and elaborate ring, belongs to the same period. It is very unlikely that the original one would have had to be replaced before 1540, and if it had been afterwards the churchwardens' accounts would doubtless have revealed the fact.

THE CENTRAL TOWER

seems to have been the last of the great additions and alterations of the 15th century. The awkward way the western piers fit on to the nave arcades shew that the latter were built first ; and the tower cannot be earlier than the rood screen, for the unmoulded bases of the piers which join it (see Plan) were never intended to be seen. Indeed, it would appear as if the rebuilding of the tower was an after-thought. When the church was restored in 1859-60, at the south-west corner lumps of bell-metal were discovered with charred wood attached to them, which seems to prove that the old tower had been burnt down ; and this no doubt took place after the chancel and nave were altered, for the reasons already stated.

There is record of money being left for the building of the tower in 1453. The churchwardens' accounts for 1470 have the following entry, " It' paied for naill for helyng (covering) of yᵉ steple . . . . . xd." I think then we may conclude that the tower was finished about this time. Of course the work may not have been continuous during the 18 years or more.

There is little evidence to show what the old tower was like. It seems probable that the Transitional church had a tower in this position, but we cannot be certain, and it may have been later. Indeed, it would almost seem as if it had been Decorated, as it is evident that four arches of that period were erected against its four piers and placed north and south.

These were altered in a curious way after the present tower was built, and they became large flying buttresses, springing straight from the north and south walls to the tower piers (see Plate XIX.). The Decorated style of these is revealed by the sunk chamfer which is used. At first it would seem impossible to determine whether the upper parts of these semi-arches were composed of old Decorated stones used up, or of Perpendicular work with the sunk chamfer copied. The latter is the true explanation, as was ascertained by the late Mr. Stead, a Ludlow mason. He found that the same masons' marks were used on these upper stones as on the tower, whereas they are quite lacking on the lower parts of the arches. These buttresses are certainly one of the most remarkable features of the church.

This splendid tower has a very fine appearance both inside and out. It is supported by four lofty arches of almost equilateral form. The piers have bold mouldings: there are three shafts, and ogees between of the Perpendicular form, convex and concave parts being equal. The capitals are well moulded: the abaci begin with slopes and have ogees underneath; the bases are bell-shaped and the plinths octagonal. The plan of the tower is oblong at the base (see Plan), but becomes square above the arches, the north and south walls being brought forward over a bold string-course. The wooden vaulting is chiefly modern, but parts of the old vault are used.

ST. JOHN'S CHAPEL

is on the north side of the first bay of the chancel and is separated from it by a fine Perpendicular arch, moulded with the double ogee. It belonged to the Transitional church, for the same small white stone, plinth moulding, and semi-hexagonal string-course are used as we see on the rest of the work of this period. With these exceptions however there is scarcely anything to remind us that the chapel is not of the 15th century. The windows are all Perpendicular. Below the east window the wall is thinner, apparently in consequence of some internal fitting, now removed. It cannot be on account of an earlier opening, for the original string-course runs along outside at the level of the sill. The stonework of the east window has been restored. Some of the glass is also modern, but there is a good deal of the original, a beautiful work of art of the 15th century. It has already been noticed that the Palmers' Guild had considerable influence on the church of Ludlow. This window depicts the legend which is supposed to be the origin of the guild. It is described as follows by the present rector, the Rev. Prebendary Clayton:—
"The legend relates that two palmers or pilgrims from Ludlow, while on a pilgrimage to the Holy Land were on their journey benighted in a wood. There they were met by a beggar who told them he was St. John the

Evangelist, and that a little while before he had, in the same garb, asked alms from King Edward the Confessor, who having at the moment nothing else to give, bestowed on him the ring from his finger. St. John bid them return the ring to the King, and tell him that in six months after receiving it, he would be with him in paradise. This they did on their return to England. The legend certainly had its rise from some circumstance which had brought palmers from Ludlow into communication with the great Saxon King. And there is all the more interest attaching to it as it is known that a Society of Palmers did exist in Ludlow at a very early period."

The other windows have no particular connection with Ludlow, but they are very interesting all the same, especially the two which form one subject,—figures of the Apostles, each with an article of the Apostles' Creed. The other window has the Lord's Prayer, besides figures of our Lord, and several saints. It has had an inscription, but now only the words *Katharine uxoris ejus hanc fenestram fieri fecit* remain. We cannot tell who the husband was. The date of the windows is probably early in the 15th century,—Perpendicular on account of the rich yellow colour, among other things, and the forms of the lights, and early on account of the almost Decorated foliage used.

The present doorway is modern, but has been renewed I suppose on an old Perpendicular form. The staircase to the tower starts from this chapel.

The roof is chiefly remarkable for the peculiar form it assumes at the east end. It is curved quite like a baldachino, and was no doubt so arranged to form a canopy to an altar below. I do not know of any other instance of this form in mediaeval architecture. This is clearly Perpendicular, and has representations of angels and Tudor flowers.

There are two matrices on the floor from which the brass has entirely disappeared. On the south side is an elaborate Classical tomb to the memory of Sir John Bridgeman, Chief Justice of Chester, who died in 1637, and his wife, Francisca. The two effigies are of marble and are clad in the dress of the period, ruffs being still worn. The knight is not in armour, but his feet rest against a lion, the lady's against a dog.

Some old pews can be seen in this chapel. On the east wall, south of the window, is a fragment of a fresco, which evidently belonged to to the 14th century, the tracery represented being of that character. Against the east wall is a screen, which shews the linen pattern and a carved cornice. The western screen, which separates the chapel from the transept, is the finest in the church. It is coved outwards on both sides, and has tracery and panelling of Perpendicular character; some of the quatrefoils are filled with square flowers and some are open. The cornice is most beautifully carved.

There are double doors, and the whole screen is now glazed.

THE LADY CHAPEL

It has been disputed that the chapel on the south side of the chancel is the lady chapel and I must therefore prove that it is so. There can be no doubt that there was a chapel dedicated to the Virgin in St. Lawrence's church, for the churchwardens' accounts constantly refer to it. The evidence as to its position is also to be found in these important documents. In 1570, 13s. 4d. was paid for a pew, "at our Lady chauncell dore, on the south side the church." There were several chapels on the south side of the church, but I feel sure that the south aisle or the south transept cannot be here intended. If the south aisle or any part of it had been meant, the accounts of the same year would not speak of the south aisle as such, which they do. Neither can the south transept be referred to, for in 1559-60 new glass was put up, "in our Lady chauncelle in the next window to the dore upon the southe side." If this indicates a *door* on the south side, it cannot refer to the transept, for there is no door and never has been. If it speaks of a *window* in that position the words cannot possibly describe the *one* south window in the south transept. I take it then as proved that the lady chapel is that part of the church on the south side of the first bay of the chancel.

It has already been shewn that this chapel was part of the building erected in 1199. There are still some indications of this period inside as well as out. A semi-hexagonal string-course runs along the south wall, and underneath is a piscina, which bears evidence of the Transition period. The arch is semi-circular but it is not pure Norman, as there is a fillet worked on the roll. It is exactly a form we should expect at this time. The appearance of this part of the wall is very remarkable (see Fig. 19).

Fig. 19.

At a later period another piscina has been inserted a little to the east of this one. It is a beautiful specimen of the Early English style with a well moulded trefoil arch. It seems possible that this may have been originally in the Early English wall of the chancel, and removed to its present position when the chancel was altered in the 15th century. Whether this was so or not it was no doubt placed where it now is on account of an alteration of the level of the altar near. The Early English piscina is at a higher level than the Transitional one. At the same time probably, grooves were made in the latter, cutting into the roll and fillet, to place a credence shelf there. There was evidently an aumbry before these alterations took place, and the jamb with hinges remains, east of the Early English piscina.

There are no original windows in the chapel. The Jesse window in the east wall is Decorated. It is of five lights, and has reticulated tracery (see Plate XIX.). Most of the glass has been "restored," but there are fragments of the old, including four of the figures of the ancestors of our Lord. The other windows have been renewed, but the design is late Perpendicular. They must have been inserted some time after the great Perpendicular alterations, which were probably finished about 1470. The doorway under the most westerly of these windows is an ancient one as is shown by the mediaeval tiles which are found there. I suppose it was blocked when the window above was put up. The door of the lady chapel, as noticed above, is referred to in the churchwardens' accounts at a later period, but this may be the door in the screen, for it is probable that similar doors in the screens giving entrance to the chancel and St. John's chapel are mentioned. The screen here is not quite so grand as the corresponding one on the north side of the church, but it is very beautiful. The style is Perpendicular and it has tracery of that character; the upper part is coved outwards. The roof is good Perpendicular, but has not the canopy, which is such a striking feature in St. John's chapel.

The large slab on the floor of this chapel was found at the east end of the south aisle. It is about 6 ft. long by 3 ft. broad. It looks as if it might be the base of an altar, but the under edge, which can be felt at the south west corner, is smooth, which seems to indicate that it is the altar slab turned upside down. I am told, however, that there are no crosses on the underside, and the slab may be part of an altar *tomb*. Various fragments near were found in different parts of the church. There is one cross of Early English and one of Decorated character. One fragment is Perpendicular and has elaborate quatrefoils and square flowers: it is very similar to the panelling at the west end of the north aisle.

On the north side is a Perpendicular arch exactly like the corresponding one in St. John's chapel, already described. Underneath it is fixed, among other things, a board of great interest. It is a table of "The X Commandemems of almighty god" (see Fig. 20). They are considerably

Fig. 20.

shortened, and the wording is different from the version of 1611. The letters I H S can be seen and also the Tudor rose. This remarkable piece of work is evidently of the year 1561, for the accounts tell us that in March of that year a sum of money was paid for "the table of commaundementes," and in the next month we have "for settinge the table of the commaundementes in a frame." We cannot precisely fix the price, for in each case the figure mentioned includes something else. Eighteen pence was paid for the table, "and the new kalender." Three shillings was sufficient for setting up the table, and "mendynge the bellowes of the great organs, and clensinge the same, withe other worke done about the same." It is scarcely necessary to say that the apparently modest sums mentioned in the accounts would represent several times as much of our present money.

There are now no signs of the images which stood here and in other parts of the church; nor of "the seate where our Ladie stode in our Lady chaunselle," which was pulled down in 1559-60. A number of images were sold in 1548 and later. That of St. George appears to have been a particularly rich one: it fetched 1s. 6d., the "volt" that it stood in, 3s. 4d., the "lofte" that it stood on, 6s., and "the dragon that the image of saynt George stode upon . . . . vijd."

THE NORTH TRANSEPT.

I think there can be little doubt that this is St. Margaret's chapel. In 1559-60 we read of glass being set up "in saynt Margrettes chaunselle in the northe window." No chapel on the south side has a north window, and St. Margaret's must therefore be on the north side. It cannot be St.

John's chapel, and that it is no part of the north aisle is, I think, shewn by an entry of the year 1572-73, telling of "a pewe lyinge in the north ile of the churche anontes (opposite) St. Margarettes chauncelle."

This transept is often called the Fletchers' chapel, and is supposed to have been erected by a guild of arrow makers. The mark of the guild—an arrow—still appears outside on the gable.

This part of the church was no doubt erected in the latter half of the 14th century. The tracery of the original windows is of late Decorated, almost of Flamboyant character. The north window has been restored, but the old stonework was so much decayed that it is not certain that the present tracery accurately represents the original. There is one Perpendicular window, high up in the west wall. The altar was evidently under the east window. On the left are two aumbries (see Plan), and on the right a piscina. This, like the windows, has poor mouldings : the bases of the shafts in both places shew the approach of the Perpendicular style, being more or less bell-shaped. The transept was considerably heightened in the 15th century, and the roof is Perpendicular and rests on the original corbels. The screen belongs to the same period and is a very good one, though not nearly so elaborate as that near to it, at the entrance to St. John's chapel.

The organ was built by Snetzler, and was presented to the church in 1764 by the Earl of Powis : it formerly stood on the rood screen and has twice been rebuilt and enlarged.

THE SOUTH TRANSEPT.

Several entries in the churchwardens' accounts make it almost certain that this is St. Catharine's chapel. An entry of 1559-60 mentions glass "in saynt Katherne chaunselle in the southe window." This cannot well refer to any part of the south aisle, for that is mentioned by name in the same year.

The architectural character of the transept makes it probable that it was built before the middle of the 14th century. The reticulated tracery which is used in the three original windows is most common in the middle of the Decorated period. The south window has the sunk chamfer moulding on the scoinson arch : the east window contains a little 14th century glass.

Against the south wall is a monument to the memory of Lady Eure, who died in 1612. The figure reclines on the left elbow and is of alabaster : the costume is late Elizabethan. At the foot is a half-figure of a man in armour. Near this monument, which was moved from the chancel at the restoration, are two incised slabs of 17th century date.

This transept, like the other, was heightened in the 15th

century.   There is a Perpendicular window in the east wall, and the roof belongs to the same period and has the original corbels.   The screen is also Perpendicular, and is of different design from any of the others.   There is no piscina or aumbry remaining.

THE NAVE

is a most impressive piece of architecture (see Plates XVIII. and XIX.).   It is composed of six bays, and the arches are lofty and well-proportioned.   The view from the west end takes in the whole length of the church, but the detail of the chancel is rather hidden by the screen and the piers which support the central tower.   It will be noticed that the chancel bears a little to the south, but it is almost too slight to shew on the Plan.   It is difficult to say exactly where the deviation commences, but it is probably only in the three eastern bays, which were built at later periods than the main bay.

Till the alterations in the 15th century the arcade on the south side was presumably Transitional, and that on the north, Decorated. I am unable to say whether the rebuilding of the nave took place before that of the chancel or not, but it was done before the tower, as has already been stated.   There are several signs of the arcades having been rebuilt. This is most striking on the outside, as will be presently shown, but it may be mentioned here that the north arcade was rebuilt a little to the north of the older one, and, in consequence of this, the west door and window are no longer in the middle.   It is true that the present doorway is of the same period as the arcades, but it takes the place of one which was doubtless Transitional in exactly the same position : when the church was restored, the original plinth of Norman character was discovered.   The west window is of late Decorated character, but it is not certain that it represents the original form.   The glass, as well as that in the other windows of the nave and aisles, is modern, except some fragments in the north windows of the north aisle.

The churchwardens' accounts often speak of the wedding door. The position of this is doubtful, and it would take too long to detail all the evidence about it.   One or two entries imply that it was the north door, but I am nearly sure from others that it was the west.   I believe I am right in stating that in the 16th century, and earlier, part of the marriage service often took place at one of the doors, and thus the name. The part near it seems to have been called the wedding chapel ; for in 1563 we read of "the glasse window in the wen' chauncelle," "wen'" being apparently a contraction of "wedding."

The arches and piers are thoroughly Perpendicular.   The latter are diamond shaped, and have four engaged shafts, which are moulded

LUDLOW.
LOOKING EAST.

similarly to those on the tower piers, only less elaborately. Between these shafts a wave moulding runs all round the arch of a characteristic Perpendicular form, the concave parts being well defined. The clerestory has six windows on either side of simple design.

The roof is an excellent one, and is of the 15th century : it rests on wooden corbels. The colouring is modern, but traces of original colour were discovered on this and all the other roofs of the church, when the restoration took place.

It is known that Beaupie's chapel was in some part of the nave, for there is record of priests being appointed early in the 16th century to "Beaupie's Chantry at the altar of St. Mary and St. Gabriel the Archangel in the nave." The accounts of 1548 tell of the sale of "a image of Jhesus that stode in Beawpie chapelle." Leland speaks of the founder as "Beauvie or Beaufrie, sometime cofferer to King Edward the fourth." Churchyard, the poet, says that he was buried "full nere the font, upon the foremost side." St. Steven's chapel, we learn from the accounts of 1554-55, was "in the lower end of the churche."

THE NORTH AISLE

was built or rebuilt in the early Decorated period, and is, architecturally, chiefly remarkable for a row of six two light windows in the north wall. The sub-arches are cusped, and in the heads are circles enclosing cinquefoils. The heavy mullions have fillets worked on them. Each scoinson arch has the characteristic sunk quarter-round moulding occurring twice. Most fortunately the stonework of these windows has remained quite untouched since the early part of the 14th century, and they constitute one of the most charming features in the church (see Plates XVIII., XIX., and XX.). The window at the west end has been renewed, but it retains its original form of four lights under a segmental pointed arch, with the ball-flower profusely used (see Plate XXI.).

At the east end of the north wall are a few large stones high up, which may have belonged to an older church : there are others above the south arcade of the nave. The roof is plain and of the Perpendicular period. Near the doorway in the north wall is a stoup with the Perpendicular double ogee moulding. The doorway is original and has a roll and fillet moulding.

I do not think that any part of this aisle can be identified with the various chapels, whose position has not been already fixed. There are two aumbries at the east end of the north wall, but no piscina. At the west end of this wall is a remarkable feature which should be noted. It is a large double recess in the wall (see Plan), partly underneath the most westerly of the early two-light windows. It is highly ornamented in the Perpendicular style with elaborate quatrefoil panelling, cusped arches, crockets, buttresses, and Tudor rose. There is no altar, piscina, or any other clue to the original purpose of this remarkable feature. It may have been part of the ornamental work of one of the unidentified chapels, but we cannot be certain. It is generally supposed that it is the tomb of Prince Arthur, eldest son of Henry VII. We know that this prince died at Ludlow castle and that his bowels were buried in St. Lawrence's church, but I think the evidence is against this being the place of interment. In 1684 Thomas Dinely wrote an account of the progress of Henry, first Duke of Beaufort, through Wales. He mentions that there was an inscription in the *chancel* of Ludlow church, recording the burial, and he says that it was then believed that part of the body was interred at that spot. The inscription does not distinctly state that the interment was in the chancel, but it seems probable that if the tomb had been in the north aisle the inscription would have been there also. At any rate the tradition 200 years ago is more likely to be correct than the modern opinion.

THE SOUTH AISLE

was part of the Transitional church, as has already been shewn. The south and west walls are of that period, but no details remain inside. However, the Early English style is still represented in the windows east of the porch. The tracery is Perpendicular, and has been renewed, but the original jambs remain. A roll and fillet goes round the scoinson arch, and by the face of the window are jamb-shafts. These are Early English as the bases shew: there are no water hollows, but the lowest roll is round underneath and not flat as it would have been in the Decorated style. These jambs probably belong to the same period as the addition of the two bays to the chancel. The south windows west of the porch are Decorated, but the tracery has been renewed. The west window is of five lights and Perpendicular: there are moulded shafts in the jambs and foliage on the capitals.

The presence of two piscinas one at the east end and one west of the porch shows that this aisle was partly taken up with chapels at one time. These were probably divided off by wooden screens : there are no signs of stone partitions. The recess under the window next the porch on the east side was probably not a piscina, and I am indebted to Mr. J. T. Micklethwaite, F.S.A. for the suggestion that it was a lavatory. There are other instances of lavatories within churches, and the appearance here quite bears out the theory. There are two holes inside, one for the supply pipe to come through, and one for the water to go out by : this latter is connected with a large stone outlet, which cuts into the plinth moulding of the outside

PLATE XIX.

LUDLOW.
LOOKING NORTH-EAST.

wall (see Plan). It should be remembered that this aisle was more or less shut off from the rest of the church in mediaeval times, and there is nothing so incongruous in a lavatory here as might at first be supposed. There is a stoup between this and the door.

The font is round, and is a large and very rough erection, which it is impossible to date accurately, though it may of course be Norman. It has lately been replaced in this position after having been for sometime in the lady chapel. The roof is plain and good Perpendicular (see Plate XIX.).

The south doorway is one of the most charming features in the church. It is pure Early English and beautifully moulded. A section of the arch is shewn in Fig. 14, L. There is a slender shaft on either side of the door : the base on the east side has been renewed, but after the old form, and corresponds with those of the window jambs already mentioned.

West of this is a door for the staircase leading to the upper room of the porch. There was a window for this staircase, looking into the aisle, but it is now blocked. There has apparently been a door higher up on the left. The peculiar appearance of the masonry is accounted for by the changes which took place in the Perpendicular period. It is quite evident that the aisle was heightened at that time, and the upper courses of masonry are quite different from the lower all along the wall except where the porch comes. There was no need to put new stones there, as the porch and its upper room had been built before the 15th century. This older wall was however patched with the new ashlar at that time : the appearance almost suggests that there were openings from the wall on to the aisle roof, when it was lower.

It has been mentioned that there were at least two chapels in this aisle, but the dedications cannot now be determined. There is a record of money being left to the new work of the chapel of St. Edmund the King in 1348. The only parts of the present building, the architecture of which would at all correspond with this date, are the south transept, the east window of the lady chapel, and the western windows of the south wall of the south aisle. It has been shewn that the south transept was St. Catherine's chapel, and it therefore seems not unlikely that the western part of the south aisle was the chapel of St. Edmund the King. The tracery of the windows has been renewed and the form looks a little later than that of the middle of the 14th century. Whether this is so or not, we cannot be certain to which saint the chapel was dedicated.

On the south west pier of the tower are the remains of painting, and, among other designs on the south side, there is the figure of an angel holding a shield with the Warwick arms. This east end of the south aisle is therefore, in all probability, the Warwick chapel.

The accounts of 1614-15 speak of a gallery being erected in

the south aisle by Mrs. Margaret Greene, who was "purposed at her owne
cost & charges to erect and Build a gallery and to bestow it one the
schoolemaster & usher successively & to the schollers and younger sort of
people & to others wch wante pewes in the church." The scholars' chancel
is mentioned as early as 1571-72, but it is also referred to after the erection
of this gallery, and we may therefore suppose that the south aisle or part of
it went by that name.

There were enormous galleries on both sides of the church till
the restoration of 1859-60. I do not think that we can tell from the
accounts exactly when all these were erected, but we know they were
rebuilt and enlarged in 1749, according to a decision of a parish meeting of
Dec. 26th, 1748.

THE PORCH

was built in the early Decorated period, and is a beautiful hexagonal
erection. The north and south sides are taken up with the two doorways.
The sides next the inner door have square-headed panels of three divisions,
and the remaining sides have acutely pointed three-light windows, the early
geometrical tracery of which (see Plate XXI.) has been renewed. The
vaulting is excellent, though of rough material. It is sexpartite, springing
from the six corners: there are ribs along the ridges and all the ribs meet
in the centre (see Plan).

There is an architectural puzzle in this porch, which at first
appears insoluble. At a low level on the outside wall, and underneath the
windows, runs the plinth moulding shewn in Fig. 14, G. It is on both sides,
and runs round all the buttresses, except the smaller ones at the south-east
and south-west corners. This bell-shaped moulding is a thoroughly
Perpendicular form, and, though it may occur as soon as the middle of the
14th century, it is *never* seen in the early Decorated period. Yet the windows
above, and, more remarkable, the vaulting belong to that period. Strange
though it may appear, the explanation is that the porch—windows, vaulting
and most of the walls—was rebuilt in the Perpendicular period. This is
partly shewn by the different masonry used above the two lowest courses
of stones inside. However, there is a more convincing proof than this.
Mr. J. T. Irvine tells me that when the church was restored in 1859-60 he
found pieces of 14th century glass used as wedges in the ribs of the vaulting.
This seems pretty sure proof that the very unusual event of the rebuilding
of vaulting in an early form took place after the 14th century. Without
this important piece of information, I should hardly have ventured to say
that the porch had been rebuilt. It is very encouraging to find that a
valuable rule as to distinction of styles holds in this case as well as others.
Some rules of course are only general ones and must be applied with caution,

LUDLOW.

FROM THE NORTH-WEST.

but others are invariable, and under this head may be included the rule that the bell-shaped moulding of Fig. 14, G does not occur so far back as the *early* Decorated period.

The upper room existed in the original porch and does not date merely from the time of the Perpendicular rebuilding. This is shewn by the character of the masonry on the north side. The old small stone is used high up and not the large Perpendicular ashlar. I can find no sure evidence about the use of this room in the middle ages. In the 16th century it was the deacon's chamber, which is mentioned by the churchwardens in 1545, 1559, 1569, and 1594-95. The last of these entries is decisive, for it speaks of "the deacons chamb' over the churche porche." At a later period the purpose of this room was altered, for in 1626 we read that a grant for repairing the chamber over the porch was ordered to make "a sufficient place for a librarie, according to the Lord Bishoppes graunt & desire."

THE EXTERIOR

is chiefly remarkable for the splendid tower, the landmark for miles around (see Plates XX. and XXI.). It is 166 feet in height, only 34 feet short of the tower and spire of Worfield (see Plate XII.). The stone was so badly worn that it was necessary to recase it a few years ago: a beautiful local red sandstone was used. Most of the details are reproductions of the old forms, but the figures had long disappeared, and the present ones do not therefore represent the originals. The windows are of a rather late form,—of four lights with two divisions in each: the heads are four-centred arches and there is very little tracery. The tower is finished with four good pinnacles and a battlement.

There have at one time been pinnacles all along the nave and chancel. Most of these have disappeared entirely, one or two have been restored, and there are one or two of debased character, such as those at the south-west corner (see Plate XXI.). There are constant references in the churchwardens' accounts to the repairing and rebuilding of pinnacles. I cannot refrain from quoting an amusing entry in this connection. "Memorand' that it is ordered & agreed uppon by the Churchwardens & other of the parish of Ludlow the 27 day of ffeay 1630 that at the request of Mr Tho: Colbatch Parson of the same that the said parish from time to time heerafter shall save & harmelesse keepe the said Tho: Colbatch from all damages that shall heerafter happen unto him from the fall of one pinacle that is loose over the highe Chauncell or by any other casualty that may come from the Steeple of the said Church unto the Chauncell wch the Parson for the time beinge is under to repaire." The good rector, it would appear, could not induce the churchwardens to do their duty in keeping the tower in repair, but he guarded himself against having to expend money on the *chancel* through the fall of another part of the building.

The buttresses against the clerestory walls are evidently of the same debased period or periods as the pinnacles : a whitish stone is used, quite different from the red stone of the 15th century.   On the north side of the south clerestory wall at the top are the remains of an inscription in difficult 15th century letters, which were so worn in 1859-60 that nothing could be made out from them.

I have already mentioned the Perpendicular plinth moulding on the porch.   It runs round all the buttresses, except the smaller ones at the south east and south west corners (see Plan).   However, these buttresses were built at the same time as the others as can be seen by the way the stones are bonded.   The stonework of the door has been renewed : it has the sunk chamfer moulding, and the hood shewn in Fig. 14, E.   For some time before the restoration there was a door to the turret staircase from the outside.   The battlement of the porch and the quatrefoil band below have been renewed.   The window over the door looks more like Perpendicular than early Decorated, but the stone is new.   The figure below of the Good Shepherd and also the niche are modern.

The south wall of the south aisle is of the Transition period. The semi-hexagonal string-course and plinth moulding (Fig. 14, B and A) will be noticed.   Near the chimney for the warming apparatus at the north east corner of the porch is one of the early buttresses, quite of Norman character (see Plan).   A little farther east the basement moulding is interrupted by the outlet of the lavatory inside the south aisle.   In the window above is part of the jamb of an Early English window (see Plan). The form of it shews us plainly that there was a pair of lancets in this position, and no doubt the same form was used farther east.   In each case the intervening masonry has been removed to make a three-light Perpendicular window.   The greatly projecting buttresses of the south aisle are of course not original : they were added in the Perpendicular period. The masonry all along should be observed : the lower part is early and of small stones, the upper being Perpendicular with large ashlar.

This heightening of the walls in the 15th century also took place in the south transept.   The lower part here is similar to that of the south aisle and makes one inclined to think that the transept was not first of all built in the Decorated period, but was rebuilt with older stones at that time.   The plinth moulding has the string-course of Fig. 14, A, but not the slope below : this is indicated on the Plan by one line being drawn instead of two.   The moulding is continued round the corner buttresses, which are diagonal—a sufficient proof that the transept cannot be Transitional.

Underneath the windows is the string-course shewn in Fig. 14, E, considerably decayed in parts. This is a characteristic Decorated form,—the scroll and a small round below.

The double plinth moulding begins again on the south wall of the lady chapel, is interrupted by the doorway now blocked, and goes round another flat buttress belonging to the church of 1199. The other buttresses are additions, doubtless of the late Perpendicular period, when the windows were inserted : one of these rests on an early sepulchral cross. The south and east walls of the chapel have been almost entirely refaced and many of the details renewed, including a semi-hexagonal string-course which runs round : this is an unusual feature in Perpendicular moulding, but it is of a different form from that in the early work, being of greater projection.

I have already referred at length to the character of the junction of the lady chapel with the south wall of the chancel. The base moulding of the former is continued right past that of the latter, shewing that the chancel wall is later, though the actual form of the moulding is the same. This moulding is continued along the chancel for nearly two bays and then stops abruptly (see Plan). We should gather from this that the eastern bay is later. The matter was absolutely settled in 1859-60 by Mr. J. T. Irvine, who discovered the foundation of a corner buttress in this position. No signs of this appear above the ground, but Mr. Irvine tells me that he thinks there were two buttresses, at right angles to one another, and not *one* corner-wise. This would quite fit in with the Early English date I have assigned to the two bays. At any rate it conclusively proves that the chancel at one time ended here. It is clear on the exterior, as it was inside the chancel, that the Early English part was considerably rebuilt in the 15th century. The south wall of the eastern bay is exclusively Perpendicular as are the buttresses. At a low level the string course shewn in Fig. 14, H is used, and under the windows that in Fig. 14, K.

These same mouldings are used on the east wall, and the former runs round the buttresses. These buttresses, with their pedimented heads and few stages, look Early English at first sight, but their 15th century date is established by the characteristic string-course referred to, and by the elaborate multifoil panel enclosing a shield, remains of which, more or less imperfect, can be seen on each of the eastern buttresses. The east wall, which has several putlog holes, is thoroughly Perpendicular with two exceptions. One is the low side-window (see Fig. 15) already dealt with, and the other is the pear moulding under the great window, which, like the jambs inside, was originally used in the Early English work.

This pear moulding is also seen under the most easterly of the northern windows. The vestry has no plinth moulding. A great deal of rubbish has been cleared away from around it, as well as from other walls of the church. The churchwardens' accounts often speak of the removal of "ramel."

The Transitional work again appears on St. John's chapel. There is the semi-hexagonal string-course, and the plinth moulding below. The buttresses are Perpendicular additions. The east wall is almost entirely original, but the north wall was re-faced in the 15th century on the outside from the window sills upwards, at the same time being reduced in thickness.

In the east wall of the north transept is a sloping stone which looks as if it had been the pitch of a former roof. I do not see what this can mean. It cannot be part of an older roof of St. John's chapel, as the transept is a much later building. At this height it can hardly refer to a pentise over a porch: it is perhaps merely a chance position of a particular stone. The transept is late Decorated, except the upper Perpendicular walls, and a return has taken place to the older disposition of corner buttress, two being placed at right angles, and not one diagonally, as in the middle Decorated south transept. There are clear indications that the north transept is later than St. John's chapel and the north aisle at the point where it joins them. The same plinth moulding, viz., that in Fig. 14, A, is used on nearly all the parts of this church before the 15th century; but there are breaks in this case. The moulding on St. John's chapel in carried past that on the transept, and on the west side the transept moulding is higher than that of the aisle. The former arrangement is shewn on the Plan, but it is impossible to represent the latter. The arrow on the gable has already been mentioned.

The six early Decorated windows of the north aisle look very charming from the outside. The tracery is worn, but still has some vitality: the hood-mouldings have decayed considerably. The buttresses are quite of Decorated character, with breadth equal to projection. Their date is still further revealed by the scroll string-course, shewn in Fig. 14, D. This should be compared with the similar form on the south transept, E, and particularly with that on the north transept, F. The moulding on the aisle is larger and rather more oval in form. This last characteristic shews the nearness of the Early English period, as we might expect in *early* Decorated work: in the 13th century the scroll, when used, is often of an elliptical contour. The upper part of the wall has the 15th century ashlar, but it is only a refacing, the wall inside being the same throughout except the few large stones that were re-used. The Perpendicular builders retained the beautiful early ball-flower string-course. The north doorway is original: it has a wave moulding of Decorated character. The hood moulding has apparently been removed, but its form is such as might be

LUDLOW.
FROM THE SOUTH-WEST.

used at the beginning of the 14th century, as the scroll moulding is combined with undercutting. At the side of the door are pieces of masonry, which look like parts of shafts, but they are merely the returns of the plinth moulding. There is the mark of the roof of a low-pitched porch. I am not sure whether or not this is the leaden porch, referred to in the churchwardens' accounts : there may perhaps have been one to St. John's chapel, and there certainly was one at the west end of the nave.

The west wall presents a somewhat patched appearance and has stonework of at least five periods. The lower part of the end of the nave and almost all the end of the south aisle are Transitional. The west wall of the north aisle is early Decorated in its lower part, and contains the four-light window already referred to with its renewed ball-flower ornament (see Plate XXI.). The upper part belongs to a debased period : it is of the same stone as the debased buttresses against the clerestory walls. The stonework about the large west window of the nave is probably of the same date as the erection of the window—the latter part of the 14th century. Perpendicular ashlar is seen at the very top of the south aisle wall, and in a peculiar manner in two strips up the nave wall. This shews us that when the nave arcades were rebuilt they were carried right through the older wall.

The position of the earlier arcades is evidently fixed to a certain extent by the flat buttresses, the remains of which are seen on either side of the west door. The Perpendicular architects rebuilt the north arcade a little nearer the north wall than it was before, and set the buttress against it. It appears that they intended to build the south arcade in a corresponding position, for the buttress on that side is about the same distance south of the door as the other one is north. Curiously enough they changed their minds, and rebuilt the south arcade pretty much in its original position. The buttress therefore, as shewn on the Plan, is not directly opposite the arcade.

In consequence of the alteration in the position of the north arcade, the doorway and window above are no longer in the middle of the nave. Even since this alteration, the north aisle is a little wider than the south. An unsymmetrical arrangement was started when the early Decorated north aisle was built wider than the Transitional south aisle. The Perpendicular builders intended to keep the position of the nave symmetrical and to reduce the aisles, but they changed their minds, contracting the north aisle to almost the same width as the south, and, as a necessary penalty, leaving the nave unsymmetrical with regard to the

west door and window.   At the same period apparently the end wall of
the nave became thinner than that of the aisles (see Plan).

The west doorway has been renewed after the Perpendicular
form : there are no signs of the plinth of Norman character discovered in
1859-60. Besides the Transitional buttresses already named, there are slight
remains of others against both the south-west corner buttresses.   In the end
wall of the south aisle are some marks which may indicate the position of
a former window, placed high up to light a gallery.

The west front is of a strikingly varied character like the rest
of this remarkable building, a building which in architectural, antiquarian,
and artistic interest is equalled by few parish churches in Shropshire or
any other county.

LUDLOW.
St. Mary Magdalene.

Ludlow.

St. Mary Magdalene.

HE chapel in Ludlow castle is not a parish church, but I describe it here on account of its remarkable character. It is one of the five round churches of mediaeval date which remain in England, the others being at Cambridge, Northampton, Little Maplestead, and the Temple Church in London. The chapel is pure Norman and was probably erected in the reign of Henry I. There is the foundation of a small rectangular projection on the east side for the chancel, which however may have extended farther eastward : an old print shews the building continued to the wall of the castle.

The doorway on the west (see Plate XXII.) is ornamented with round billets and zig-zags, with stars on the abaci, and frets and scolloping below. The string-course above the door, which goes round the building, has a double row of round billets. There are three Norman windows high in the wall. The one over the doorway is ornamented with scolloping, and the billet and zig-zag : the other two are plain. That on the north was adapted at a later period for a door with a depressed arch, which communicated with a passage leading to the living apartments of the castle. At the same time an upper floor of some kind was made to the chapel, supported on a peculiar assortment of corbels, some or all of which are of 13th century character : one has the mask ornament and another is an Early English capital with undercut abacus. It is impossible to say exactly how far this floor extended across the building, but it was apparently a narrow gallery going round the circular part of the chapel, and terminated by the jambs of the chancel arch : the marks evidently indicate this. The level of the floor is not precisely the same on the two sides of the arch : it is not difficult to imagine that a slight mistake might be made in carrying a gallery round the building. I think that this difference in the level of the marks shews us that they do not indicate the position of a rood beam, as might be supposed at first sight. If a beam had been placed across such a comparatively narrow arch, care would no doubt have been exercised to keep it horizontal.

It was of course no uncommon thing to have an upper floor to a chapel in a mediaeval house, and the term "solar" was sometimes applied to it. At Ludlow the arrangement did not exist in Norman times: judging by the depressed arch, the change must have taken place in the Tudor period. The gallery would darken the lower part of the chapel, and two square-headed windows, each of two lights, were added. There were no windows low down originally, but an ornamental arcade, with seven arches on each side of the doorway. The arches have round and zig-zag mouldings alternately, and scolloping and volutes on the capitals.

The chancel arch is recessed, tall, and handsome: it has a peculiar twist to adapt it to the circular wall. The ornamentation is elaborate: the hood-moulding is a double row of round billets, next is the zig-zag, and the soffit of the inner arch is covered with the star ornament. There are four shafts with scolloped capitals, the necks of which display the cable moulding. The original roof of the chapel would probably be conical, but at some late period a poor battlement has been placed on the top of the wall.

The round building which has been described is certainly later than the early Norman keep of the castle, and we naturally look for any signs of an earlier chapel. There are some ornamental arches in one of the lower rooms of the keep, and it has been supposed that this was the original chapel, but there is no proof of it.

Another chapel in the castle was founded by Roger Mortimer in the reign of Edward II., and dedicated to St. Peter. There are some remains of the chapel on the south side of the castle yard: one window is Decorated and doubtless original, and there is a later arch of Perpendicular character.

Munslow.

St. Michael.

THE church of this parish at the time of Domesday book was situated at Aston Munslow, one mile south of the present building. It must have been moved in the 12th century, for part of the church is of Norman date. The building of this period apparently consisted of chancel, nave, and western tower, but it is doubtful if anything but the tower remains. The chancel must date from the 13th century if not earlier. In the early Decorated period the south wall of the nave appears to have been rebuilt, and in the 15th century an aisle was added on the north side. A vestry was also erected, south of the chancel, in the Perpendicular period.

THE CHANCEL.

The most ancient detail of the chancel is the narrow deeply splayed window in the south wall, now blocked on account of the vestry. The east window has been renewed and filled with poor glass. In the north wall is a broad lancet without cusps, and also an uncusped two-light window of very peculiar and ugly design: both apparently date from the 14th century, but they are of nondescript character. There is a piscina in the south wall with the remains of a drain. A monument commemorates John Lloyd, the last rector before the Reformation. There are two chairs of 17th century date: the roof is chiefly modern.

The vestry is entered by a modern shouldered arch: it has a square headed window of two lights in the south wall. The most interesting feature is a very fine chest of the 14th century: it is elaborately carved with quatrefoils and flowers. Chests of this date are by no means common.

THE NAVE.

The eastern arch separating the nave from the aisle is modern and so is the chancel arch. In mediaeval times there were apparently no moulded arches in these positions, and the reason seems to be that they were hidden to a great extent by a large rood loft. The staircase, which still remains in the south wall, is not as usual at the extreme east end of the nave, but a little farther down the church. It seems probable that the loft extended from here to the chancel arch, and at the height of the top of the single light window in the south wall, which has a wooden head. The two doors from the staircase remain and have depressed arches, the erection of the loft no doubt taking place in Perpendicular times. In the wall near is a corbel of the same period with an angel holding a shield. Farther west is an early Decorated window, the head being composed of a quatrefoil within a circle (see Fig. 21). Beyond this

Fig. 21.

is another opening in the same style with a trefoil at the top : the surrounding masonry is somewhat rude. The other window in this wall is of plain character, but contains some interesting fragments of glass. One of these dates from the 14th century, and is a representation of the Virgin and Child. Another below has the same subject, but is of larger size and later date. The sill of the window is formed by an elaborate cross which cannot be much earlier than the window itself.

A reference to Plate XXIII. will shew that the tower arch is not in the middle of the nave. The position of the chancel arch roughly, but not exactly, corresponds with this. The explanation appears to be that more room was desired at the beginning of the 14th century and that the south wall was rebuilt farther outwards. However, the appearance is rather puzzling and I am not certain that the south wall is not Norman. There is no detail of that period, but the awkward way in which one of the early Decorated windows fits into the wall rather suggests that it is an insertion.

PLATE XXIII.

MUNSLOW.

The tower arch has been depressed by its load. It is plain, but rather late Norman, having a sort of leaf ornament on the hood-moulding, which terminates in heads, one of which is original.

There is a good octagonal font, which has several Perpendicular characteristics. Some of the quatrefoils are rounded and some pointed, and most are filled with flowers or shields. There are ten fine old oak seats with fret and other ornaments. The roof is good and has tie and collar beams.

THE AISLE

is separated from the nave by three wide arches, one of which is modern, and a small arch also modern. The columns (see Plate XXIII.), are moulded, and reveal the Perpendicular period : the abacus begins with a slope and has an ogee underneath, and the base is bell-shaped. There is no column at the west end of the arcade. There are three remarkable windows in the aisle, of unusual form. Each is of three lights, with spherical triangles in the head, and is contained by a trefoiled arch of graceful form and bold moulding (see Plate XXIII.). These windows must be Decorated, and rather early in the style, and yet the aisle is Perpendicular, if we may judge from the columns. The explanation I suppose is that they were originally in the north wall of the nave and moved to their present position when the aisle was built. This was not a rare alteration : I have noticed a clear case of it at Claverley (see p. 13). There is one window in the north wall of the same period as the aisle itself. It is of two lights, with a sexfoil in the head, the Perpendicular date being revealed by the vertical lines in the tracery and the hollowed mullions. The window near this is a debased one, without cusps, and belongs to the 16th century or later. Some of the glass is modern, but a good deal of it is ancient and was inserted in the 16th century. The east window is to the memory of "Richard Schepard and Joane his wyff:" the glass in the north Decorated window has the inscription :—"Of y^r charytye pray for the soul and state of Johne Lloydde which glasing was done at hys cost." The glass is probably German : it displays an anagram on the Trinity—one of the peculiar puzzles which were fashionable at the period.

There is an aumbry at the east end of the north wall, and another small recess under the debased window. There are some bits of 17th century carving, and three curious memorial tablets of dates 1602, 1674, and 1689. The roof is a poor one : its rafters are trussed, with seven cants.

THE EXTERIOR.

The view of the church from the south is delightful (see Fig. 21).

The porch is a charming 14th century erection with good Decorated tracery in wood : the barge board has been renewed. The inner doorway is of no special interest, but it is not Norman, and, combined with the other features of the wall, it seems to shew as before mentioned that the Norman wall was rebuilt further to the south in the early Decorated period. East of the windows of this date, a projection will be noticed (see Fig. 21), which has the appearance of a late Norman buttress. It is of course for the staircase to the rood loft, and is evidently an addition, as the stones do not bond in with those of the wall. The upper part of this wall is much thinner than the lower part, and may have been added when the roof was erected.

The south door to the chancel is apparently an insertion of the latter part of the 14th century : its hood-moulding is broadly hollowed in the Perpendicular manner, but the characteristic Decorated sunk chamfer is used on the jambs.

The east and north sides have no features of special interest that have not been already described.

The lower part of the tower is late Norman, and has the base moulding which is shewn in Fig. 14, A, and which began to be used at that time. The west window (see Plate XXIII.) is an insertion of the 14th century, with tracery and a. wave moulding of Decorated character. Some of the small Norman windows remain, but the upper part of the tower is much later with broad single lights and no details to reveal its date accurately.

In the churchyard, over the tomb of a former rector, there is a large canopy, which was apparently part of a lych gate.

The communion plate is of no special interest : a flagon dates from 1689. The parish register goes back to 1559.

Onibury.

St. Michael.

HERE is a mention in Domesday book of a priest of Onibury, and it seems probable that a church existed there in Saxon times. Part of the present building dates from the 12th century or earlier, but most of the detail is Early English or Decorated, and the tower at the west end of the aisleless nave is probably an addition of the 14th century.

The chancel is nearly as long as the nave and a little narrower. The east wall has three lancets under one head and an aumbry. The north wall has no windows, but there are two lancets of the usual Early English form in the south wall. The piscina has a deep basin and the stone shelf remaining. There is a monument to the memory of Dorothy Pytt, who died in 1657: it has very ugly obelisks and balls. The priest's door, which is blocked, is Early English, as is shewn by the undercut dripstone. West of this is a single-light window with a cusped arch: the transom across is not ancient. Near this window is a portion of a string course, which is of a common Norman form, as far as can be observed now that it is covered with wash. It is important to notice that this is at a lower level than the impost of the chancel arch, and is not connected with it, as we might expect. We seem to learn two things from this string-course: first, that the south-west end of the chancel, and probably, as there is no sign of an extension, the whole of the eastern part of the building, is Norman, all the windows being insertions; second, that the chancel arch· is probably of a different period from the string-course. But, it will be urged, the arch is undoubtedly Norman! It certainly appears to be, but let us examine it closely. It is semi-circular and ornamented with zig-zags of various sizes, pellets and beads. We are generally accustomed to regard these as pure Norman ornaments, but Mr. Park Harrison has lately shewn us in *Archaeologia Oxoniensis* (Supplement to Part II., 1893) that all these ornaments were used in pre-Conquest architecture. The moulding of the impost is slight, but of a form that is often seen in Saxon work. I give no illustration of the arch, as the detail is considerably hidden by yellow wash. The height is greater than is usually the case in a small Norman church, the impost being nearly ten feet from the floor, whereas Saxon arches are often lofty. However, on the whole I think the arch is Norman, though I dare not say definitely that it is not Saxon. Our knowledge of pre-Norman architecture is not so accurate as we should like it to be, and it is much to be hoped that more light will be thrown upon the subject. It is certainly a mistake to suppose, with a former generation of antiquaries, that all Saxon work was rude and clumsy.

The chancel arch has no feature in the church to correspond with it: if Saxon, it would probably be the only remains of an earlier church. It has been shewn that part or all of the chancel is Norman, but the nave has no detail earlier than the 14th century. There is a Decorated window in the south wall with a pointed arch inside, and a square head outside. The tracery has disappeared from a window in the north wall. The other windows have no beauty or interest.

The font has an octagonal stem supporting a circular basin, and has been partly renewed. The pulpit is carved with tracery and the linen pattern, but does not belong to any of the pure Gothic periods. The nave roof is a tie-beam one ; that of the chancel is plastered.

The tower is entered by a low arch under a western gallery. It has plain cusped single lights and is probably Decorated, though the name is rather a misnomer in this as in many other cases, for the work is very plain, not to say coarse in character.

The north doorway of the nave is blocked, and the south doorway has been modernised. The porch is chiefly remarkable for its trefoil arch in wood, and good cusped barge-board : it probably dates from the 14th century.

The parish register commences in 1578.

Richard's Castle.

All Saints.

THIS is one of the finest modern churches in the county, and, when it is stated that the architect was Mr. Norman Shaw, it will be easily understood that the church is remarkable.

The old parish church of Richard's Castle, of the Norman and later periods, is situated in Herefordshire. The new church is, however, at the village of Batchcott in Shropshire, and must therefore be mentioned in this work. It was given to the parish by Mrs. Johnson Foster and her two daughters, in memory of the late Mr. J. J. Foster and his eldest daughter. The church was consecrated in 1891.

The style of the building may be described as middle Decorated, but no mediæval type is exactly copied.

It consists of chancel ; nave and south aisle ; vestries ; and tower and porch on the south side. The interior effect is a striking one. The chancel is raised considerably above the nave and is highly ornamented : the ball flower is plentifully used both here and round some of the windows. The nave is separated from the aisle by a fine arcade of three bays with good moulding on the capitals and bases.

The chief peculiarity of the exterior is the position of the tower, which has, at first, the appearance of being entirely detached, but is really connected with the aisle by a low porch. The ground slopes away on the south, and a good deal of dignity is added to the appearance by the bold flight of steps, by which the main doorway is approached under the tower. The north side is less pleasing, and has a very bare look. Of course a good effect can sometimes be gained by a blank surface of wall, but one cannot help thinking that this idea is somewhat overdone here : one sadly misses the string-courses, which would nearly always have been used in mediæval times to relieve the monotony. There is no clerestory, and one does not quite see the object of making the chancel windows square-headed. These however may be matters of opinion : there can be little doubt that a noble building has been erected here by a great architect.

Rushbury.

St. Peter.

RUSHBURY church is not mentioned in Domesday book, but it was no doubt founded previously, and part of the present building, as we shall see presently, probably dates from pre-Norman times. On the whole the church is a charming, if somewhat plain, example of the Transition from Norman to Early English, and consists of nave, chancel, western tower, south porch and modern vestry.

The east front is a typical and beautiful specimen of its period (see Plate XXIV.). It displays three lancets, the central one a little longer than the others, and a circular window above. There are shafts internally to the lancets: the abaci are square and moulded in the Norman manner, but an undeveloped type of Early English foliage appears on the capitals below. The north and south walls each have a fine series of four splayed lancets, and below all these windows runs a string-course of a common Norman form. This course has been cut into near the east ends of the north and south walls respectively, but I cannot explain why: the break seems to be too far from the east wall to have been caused by a reredos and too near it for a screen. The small vestry is modern, but the opening into the chancel is the original priest's doorway. It has a pointed arch, and Norman mouldings to the hood and imposts.

There is some very good woodwork in the church. Several pews in the chancel are finely carved, dating probably from the early part of the 17th century. The nave roof has tie and collar beams: there is one purlin on each side and small braces below. The chancel roof is more elaborate, and a really fine example of a hammer-beam roof. There are four trusses with hammer-beams, and collar braces forming four-centred arches; the spandrels are filled with quatrefoils and other designs. The purlins are four in number and the braces take the form of quatrefoils. The truss at the west end of the chancel is more highly ornamented than the others: it now marks the division between nave and chancel, but this may have been in a different position before the present roof was erected in the latter part of the Perpendicular period.

PLATE XXIV.

RUSHBURY.

In the south wall of the nave is a narrow recess, which has been a square-headed window. I suppose it dates from mediæval times, but the object of it is not apparent. It is farther west than low side-windows generally are. The other windows of the nave which have not been mentioned are modern, but I cannot find out if they represent old forms. The church was restored about 1855. The font is a plain circular erection, which may be of early date. The north and south walls of the church, especially of the chancel, lean considerably outwards (see Plate XXIV.). The tower arch is of Transitional character: it is pointed and recessed, and the moulding of the imposts is Norman. The west window is a deeply splayed lancet.

The main south doorway has the same hood-moulding as the priest's doorway, and is once recessed. The shafts have been renewed but the bases are original with small water hollows, and the capitals with undeveloped foliage ending in small volutes. The porch is probably of the same date as the roofs of nave and chancel: it has some ornamental panelling, but a good deal has been renewed.

The best view of the exterior of the church is from the north-east: nearly all the detail which is visible belongs to the Transition period. Some vestiges of earlier work should, however, be carefully noticed. The western part of both north and south walls of the nave for about 40 ft. is evidently of a different period from the rest. There is herring-bone masonry low down on both sides, and on the north are some fragments of Roman work. This latter fact need not surprise us, as there was probably a Roman station at Rushbury. There is no sure indication of Saxon building in the features just mentioned, but the north doorway has an early appearance. It has a plain tympanum with a faint trellis ornament at the bottom, but the sides are not composed of long and short work. There is no certain proof that these parts of the walls are pre-Norman, but I think it is very likely that they are. Immediately east of the old work on the north side the wall becomes a little thinner, and the lancets already mentioned begin, with a string-course below them. There are several broad buttresses of Early English form, but the stonework appears to be modern. At the south-east corner the stone is worn away, by sharpening weapons it is supposed. Perhaps the mischief was done by a tombstone carver, as at Cardington (see p. 78).

The tower is of plain Transitional character: the battlement has been added at a later period, and there have been pinnacles which have now disappeared. The old pitch of the nave roof can be observed against the east wall.

The parish registers begin at the unusually early date of 1538: they are not quite perfect between 1544 and 1685, but are complete since then.

Stanton Long.

St. Michael.

IN 1081 the church of this parish appears to have been at Patton, but a century afterwards we read of a chaplain of Stanton. There is a tradition that there was a church at Brockton in the parish, and a field there is still called "Chapel Field," and has a mound in it.

Some portions of the present church evidently date from the end of the 12th or the early part of the 13th century. Some 50 years later it seems to have been necessary to rebuild the south and east walls of the chancel. In the 14th century part of the south wall of the nave was renewed, and the north wall was rebuilt at some unknown period. The porch is an addition to the original building, and the vestry was erected in 1871, the church having been restored in 1869-70 under the direction of Mr. S. Pountney Smith.

It is a well-known fact that early mediæval roofs were often insufficiently tied, and there is a good illustration of this in the chancel of Stanton Long. The north wall is a very thick one and contains an original lancet, with a square head inside. The first roof thrust this wall outwards considerably, and destroyed the south wall, for it has disappeared, and its place has been taken by a thinner wall. At the same time the east wall seems to have been rebuilt: an inspection of its north end outside will shew that it is probably of a different date from the north wall. This rebuilding took place about the third quarter of the 13th century, if we may judge by the character of the two-light window in the south wall. The *vesica piscis* form is in the head, and there is an absence of cusps throughout: it is a kind of window which was used in the latter part of the Early English period and the early part of the Decorated. The east window is of a somewhat earlier type, but the stonework appears to be modern and the original may not be represented. All the glass in the church is modern. The reredos was erected in 1890.

In the south wall of the chancel is a fine canopy, with characteristic Decorated mouldings: the hood is like Fig. 14, E, and terminates in corbels, which are carved with natural leaves. West of this is a blocked priest's door, and on the east the head of a piscina in the form of a filleted trefoil arch. This may well be of the same date as the window near it, but the small arch in the north wall is probably earlier. It is a trefoil arch of steeper pitch than the other and there is no fillet. The base of the arched recess is missing, but there is a stone which is probably part of it in the eastern splay of the single light in the south wall. It is difficult to say what the small recess is for: its position was not altered when the church was restored. There are no signs of a door, and one might suppose that it was formerly a piscina in the south wall, and that it was replaced by the later one when the wall was rebuilt. It is curious, however, that the base should have been used up in the window, for that is cusped and evidently later than the piscina in the south wall. A recess was found closed up in the wall where the vestry door now is: it is replaced behind it.

The present roofs of nave and chancel probably date from the 15th century. The form is very good—collar-braced, with bold quatrefoils between the purlins, and, in the chancel, ornamental bosses on the collars. The roofs have been cut into to suit a lath and plaster ceiling. The pulpit and choir seats are partly made of oak panels of early 17th century character.

There was no chancel arch when the church was restored, and the present one is therefore modern. The northern windows of the nave are modern: there were none before 1870. The window west of the south door is modern, but the other two windows in this wall are original. One of these has two lights, and is moulded outside with the sunk chamfer, and a wave moulding of Decorated character. The mullion is partly made of a moulded stone like the jamb of the earlier two-light window in the chancel: this seems to indicate that there was another of these windows at one time. The small window in the south-east corner of the nave is also Decorated, and was no doubt inserted to light an altar, which was erected at the same time as the piscina near to it. The semi-circular form of the scoinson arch may be noted as an instance of the use of this type long after the Norman period. This south wall has two breaks in the masonry and has evidently been partly renewed: the western portion was rebuilt in 1870. The west window is a long lancet and is original. The font is round, on an octagonal stem, but the date of it is not evident.

The south doorway has a pointed arch, combined with an almost Norman moulding on the imposts. The form of chamfer termination on the jamb shews that the doorway is not pure Norman. It belongs, like the other early parts of the church, as already stated, to the Transition period. The door and its fine ironwork are evidently original: the crescent

form so common on 12th century doors, as at the Heath chapel, is giving
way to the more elaborate type of the Early English style. The porch may
have been erected at the same time as the roof of the church. The wooden
bell turret is of no particular interest.

The west wall has an original buttress of one stage under the
lancet window. The form is just what we should expect in the Transition
period, the breadth being considerably greater than the projection : a pure
Norman buttress would have been still flatter. The wall has a sloping base,
which is carried round the corners. On the north side it is soon met by
a plainer and higher plinth. This north wall is not so thick as the west,
and was evidently rebuilt at a later period. There may be little romance in
this gradual renewal of the walls on account of faulty construction, but it
is interesting to trace the rebuilding, and to suggest reasons for it. The
original church is now represented only by the north wall of the chancel,
the west and part of the south walls of the nave.

This parish has registers dating from 1568. There is a chalice
with the date 1571 on the top, which is now used as a paten.

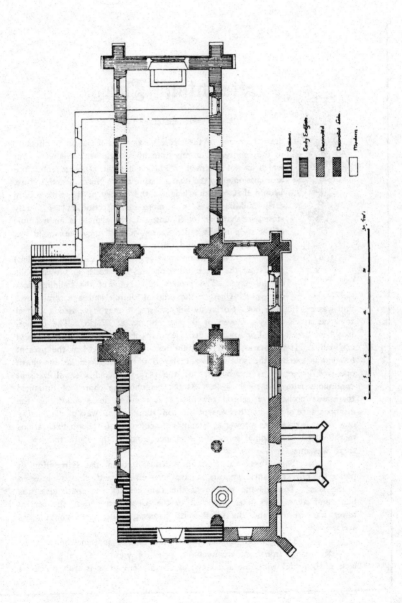

ST. AUNTON LACEY :

Saxon.
Early English.
Decorated.
Decorated late.
Modern.

Staunton Lacey.

St. Peter.

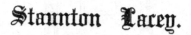

E have here one of the clearest examples of Saxon architecture in the county, or at any rate of a style which is early, but which is not Norman. This is not the place to enter into a discussion as to the nomenclature of pre-Norman architecture. Would that our knowledge of the history of these interesting early buildings was in a more exact condition! I merely state here that part of Staunton Lacey church is an example of the style usually called Saxon—a well known example too, quoted by Bloxam and other authorities.

The Saxon portions of the church (see Plan) consist of the north transept, and the north and west walls of the nave. The present appearance of the building does not reveal whether the original church had a central tower and was cruciform or not. So far as we can see, it may have had a central tower as at St. Mary's, Dover, or it may not, as at Worth. The chancel may have been apsidal or square-ended. Perhaps there was no south transept originally. If there was, it is certainly remarkable that, when the present tower was erected, the south transept should not be retained, as the north one was, especially as the builders of the period erected a small transept continuous with the south aisle. At the neighbouring church of Bromfield there was probably a central tower, and it is easy to account for the disappearance of the south transept. I can think of no way of discovering now whether there was a tower at Staunton Lacey or not, though excavations might reveal the original form of the chancel, and of the south transept if there was one.

There are no Norman remains, but in the Early English period the present chancel appears to have been erected, and windows inserted in the nave. Towards the middle of the 14th century the south aisle was built, and some years later, but still in the Decorated period, the central tower was erected, and the small south transept. The porch and vestries are modern.

The general appearance of the interior is somewhat gloomy and depressing from an architectural point of view. There is a great lack of beautiful windows, and some of the modern glass is truly dreadful!

THE CHANCEL

retains few, if any of its original Early English features inside, with the exception of the doorway to the vestry ; for the east window is modern, and most of the other windows have been renewed, presumably in the old form—double lights with trefoil heads under containing arches. The most westerly of the southern windows is cusped, and belongs doubtless to the period of the central tower. The window opposite is divided low down by a modern transom and is close to a modern arch under which the organ is placed : the window at the east end of this wall has underneath it a poor Classical monument to Elizabeth Onslowe who died in 1613. Opposite this is a cinquefoiled piscina of unusual form : it no doubt belongs to the Decorated period, but there is no means of dating it accurately.

The roof seems to be of the hammer-beam type, but is greatly hidden by plaster : the figures at the west end may not be modern, but they have been placed in this church in recent times. In the vestry is a chest dated 1660. The reredos and pulpit are carved and of stone.

The chancel arch has some interesting detail : the capitals are ornamented with the ball flower and scroll moulding, which indicate the Decorated period, but we see that it is very late in the style by the bell-shaped bases of quite Perpendicular form.

The western tower arch is the same, but those that give access to

THE TRANSEPTS

are plainer, the capitals being scarcely moulded at all.

The north transept has lofty walls, but no original features appear inside. The north window is an insertion of the Decorated period, as is indicated by the use of the sunk chamfer moulding, but the form—three uncusped lights under one head—is a very unusual one at this time : the external appearance makes one inclined to think that the original form has been altered.

The south transept is merely a continuation of the aisle. In the east wall are three uncusped lights grouped together (see Plate XXV.) As a rule one would naturally pronounce such a form to be Early English, but, remembering the unusual character of the tower windows, to be referred to presently, one is inclined to consider them Decorated, especially as the arches are not acute. If Early English, they must have been brought from elsewhere, as this is a 14th century wall.

The south window is modern : underneath is a small canopy the use of which is not apparent. There is an aumbry further east and a piscina beyond ; the basin takes the form of a narrow channel.

THE NAVE

contains no original windows. The north wall has two openings, each of two lights without cusps. They are presumably Early English, though, as will be shewn presently, a similar form was used here in the Decorated period. The west wall has a modern window high up, and below is a two-light window, cusped and square-headed, with a scoinson arch over it. It is interesting to notice that the builders of the tower pulled down a small portion of the Saxon wall, as is indicated by the bell-shaped plinth moulding at the east end of the north wall. There is the same moulding on the other side of the nave.

THE AISLE

is divided from the nave by two wide arches. The mouldings of the capitals are simple but effective: the scroll is used on the abacus and the neck, and the base is of that spreading form common during the latter half of the Decorated period, which, for want of a better name, may be called the undeveloped bell-shaped base; it approaches the Perpendicular form, which has been already described. The west window is a single cusped opening, and that in the south wall is square-headed, and of three lights with reticulated tracery. The font is either late Decorated or Perpendicular: it is octagonal and has a number of plain shields upon it.

From a cursory examination it might be difficult to tell which was first erected, the aisle, or the tower and south transept, but an examination of the evidence will make the matter clear. I have already pointed out that the bases of the aisle columns are of a somewhat earlier type than those of the responds of the tower arches. The character of the buttress at the east end of the aisle also helps us. It was of course erected to support the tower, but at first sight the presence of a plinth moulding might seem to indicate that it had been external: we have seen however that a plinth moulding is used internally in the nave on the north side. It is evident that this buttress has always been internal, for if not the (supposed) west wall of the transept must have been *east* of it, and there is no sign of this in the masonry, and also a wall in this position would not correspond with the plinth moulding outside (see Plan). If on the other hand a west wall of the transept had been *west* of the buttress, there would have been no object in the plinth moulding to the east of the eastern arch of the aisle. None of these objections can be urged against the existence of a former east wall of the *aisle*, as the tower builders would take away the portion of the wall now serving as the south-west support to the tower, rebuilding it in their own form and leaving no trace of what was there before. On the other hand it cannot be *proved* that there ever was an east wall, as there *may* have been a Saxon transept to the east of the aisle.

When we examine

THE EXTERIOR

it is again evident that the aisle and transept are not of the same period : the buttresses are different, and the plinth moulding of the transept stops at the commencement of the aisle (see Plan). The end of this plinth is cut away to fit on to the unmoulded base of the aisle wall. Such a thing would not have taken place if the transept had been earlier. As a general rule mediæval builders altered or added to a church without much considera-tion of the style of their predecessors, but it is interesting to observe that in some cases they made their own work to harmonise more or less with the earlier work it joined, and we see an example of this in the small and almost hidden plinth moulding of the south wall of Staunton Lacey. I have entered into some of these minor points here in somewhat wearisome detail, but it is necessary to examine them all carefully to prove that the aisle and transept were built at different periods and that the former is the earlier.

The central tower is massive and plain. The corbel table is simple but effective. The most remarkable feature is the character of the windows, which all have an Early English appearance, but which are certainly Decorated. Each one is composed of two lights and has no cusps. This is a good illustration of the fact that the characteristic tracery of a style often does not appear in the tower windows, and one should always be careful about dating a building by these features. In towers and unimportant positions the lancet window often occurs in the Decorated period, as at the neighbouring church of Culmington. It would seem however that at Staunton Lacey the late Decorated builders altogether preferred the uncusped light to the traceried window, as in the transepts already referred to ; and this is very unusual at the period, though there are well-known instances in the monastery kitchen at Durham, and the important church of Ottery St. Mary in Devonshire.

The original pitch of gable roofs can be seen above the present ones on the east, north and west sides. There are several proofs that the south transept roof was not at first gabled. It will be noticed (see Plate XXV.) that the pitch of the eastern roof is continued as a horizontal string along the south wall. Below this is a rough buttress, very different from the well-built buttresses which support the tower at the other corners. Also there is a sloping joint in the masonry of the east wall of the transept. These signs shew clearly that the original roof of the transept started from the horizontal string, and was a continuation of the sloping roof of the aisle. This explains the lowness of the corner buttresses (see Plate XXV.). The presence of the large window in the south wall is

STAUNTON LACEY.

no argument, as it is modern. It is evident that at some period a portion of the east wall of the transept has been removed, leaving the poor buttress already referred to, and that the south wall has been heightened to receive a gable roof.

The plinth moulding of the transept is continued a little way along the south wall of the chancel (see Plan), shewing that that small portion was rebuilt with the tower. In this wall are two canopied recesses with mutilated figures below. They are Decorated, and presumably of about the same period as the tower. The western one has ball flowers at the terminations of its dripstone, and the other has the scroll and sunk chamfer mouldings. The priest's door has a poor carved head over it, probably placed there in the late Decorated period, for there are heads in a similar peculiar position over the upper windows of the tower on the north, east, and south sides (see Plate XXV.).

The east wall has some features of interest. There are two buttresses at each corner, moulded at the base in the manner shown in Fig. 14, A. It is curious that the string-course alone is continued along the wall, and even this was evidently not intended at first, for the moulding is not bonded in to that of the buttresses : the rounded edge of the latter is continued to the east wall, past the string course which now projects from it. It may be that the wall has been built up again at some later period and the string course re-inserted : the buttresses are undoubtedly genuine. The Early English plinth is not seen on the north and south walls (see Plan).

The tower is reached by an external staircase at the north-east corner. In the north wall of the transept is the peculiar Decorated window already referred to, which has the sunk chamfer profusely used.

Attention must now be directed to the remarkable Saxon character of the walls of the north transept, and the north and west walls of the nave. On all these there are pilaster strips composed of long and short work, which is of course one of the most characteristic marks of the Saxon style. The walls are lofty, particularly the north wall of the transept, which is remarkably so. This wall shews signs of an original window, now blocked, east of the large inserted window : it was evidently not splayed externally as many Saxon windows were. High up in the gable is a similar light, which is probably not original.

Most of the pilaster strips are simply vertical, but two or three have short pieces crossing them. The north doorway, now blocked, is specially interesting (see Fig 22). It has a semi-circular head, and also the projecting masonry, acting as a hood-moulding and continued down the jambs, which is so commonly seen on Saxon doorways. Most of this is

Fig. 22.

quite square, but there is a round moulding under the hood.   The imposts
are chamfered underneath, but the characteristic quirk, or small channel, of
the Norman style (as in Fig. 10) is of course missing.   Over the doorway
is a simple Saxon cross, and above it an ornament, the lower part of which
is composed of four pellets, similar to those constantly occurring in Norman
carving.   The Saxon work at Staunton Lacey deserves careful study,
though it is not so rich or varied as that at Earl's Barton, Sompting, etc.
The presence of the chamfer below the abacus and the round below the hood
rather suggest a late date in the period—probably the time of Edward the
Confessor.

          The straight joint between the west walls of the nave and aisle
will be noticed and the corner buttress of the latter.   East of this are two
canopied recesses, later perhaps than the buttress, but still quite of Decorated
form and earlier probably than those in the chancel wall.   The sunk chamfer
occurs in the hood-moulding of one, and both have the equally characteristic
Decorated form of the sunk quarter-round, or to be more exact, in this case
an eighth of a circle, sunk—the moulding which is also used on the south
doorway.   Underneath the canopies are sepulchral crosses which may well
be of the same date.   One of them is a beautiful design, with carving of
natural foliage.   The porch is modern.
          The parish register is carried back to 1561.

Stokesay.

St. John.

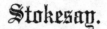

THIS church has little to recommend it from an architectural point of view, but is interesting for several reasons. The celebrated Stokesay Castle is one of the finest 13th century houses remaining in the kingdom, but there are no signs of corresponding grandeur in the church, which is quite close to it.

In the great Civil war the castle was surrendered to the parliamentary forces, and it would appear that the church was partially destroyed during the siege. At any rate it was rebuilt in 1654, and we therefore have here an interesting and rare instance of such an event taking place during the Commonwealth. Over the tower arch is the inscription

AN : DOM : 1654
THIS CHURCH WAS REBUILT BY THE
PIOUS OVERSIGHT OF
GEORGE POWELL GENT : &
GEORGE LAMBE
CHVRCHWARDENS
THIS ARCH WAS GIVEN BY
JOHN CHESHIRE JOYNER

It is evident that we must not press the word "rebuilt" too far, for the south door is undoubtedly Norman with scolloped capitals: there is MS. evidence of a church here in the 12th century.

It is doubtful too whether the chancel was rebuilt, for it retains two square-headed Perpendicular windows: it may be that "church" does not include "chancel," a usage of the word still common. I believe in some parts of the country. The latter part of the inscription is not strictly accurate. The mouldings of the arch are of the double ogee form, as used in the Decorated period—the convex part being much greater than the concave. The mouldings of the capitals however are poor and evidently were cut when the rebuilding took place. It might at first be thought that the double ogee mouldings were 17th century copies of 14th century forms, but it is clear that this is not the case when we examine the

south, west, and north (blocked) windows of the tower, and the north windows
of the nave. Here the same double ogee form is seen in the jambs, but the
head is an unmoulded semi-circle, fitting very awkwardly on to them.
This clearly shows that the jambs are composed of older stones, particularly
when we observe that the pairs of windows in the south wall of the nave
have similar semi-circular heads *without* the moulded jambs. We see then
that when the church was rebuilt in 1654 a good deal of old material was
used up.

It is scarcely likely that "John Cheshire joyner" would block
up his new arch with a gallery; and it is evident that this feature is a later
addition, when we examine the window in the wall which lights it. This
window is higher than the other one in the same wall, but the 14th century
moulded stones go up no higher, making it highly probable, if not certain,
that the height of one window was increased to fit the gallery, the old
semi-circular head being again placed on the top.

The nave is ceiled, but the chancel roof has two visible trusses.
The one which marks the division between the two parts of the church bears
the date 1664, which seems to shew that the repairs to the chancel were not
completed till ten years after the nave was rebuilt. The east window is
nondescript. The porch is very plain.

By far the most beautiful feature in the church is the large
covered pew at the entrance to the chancel. This kind of pew has generally
been swept away in modern times, and I am glad to be able to give an
illustration of one of the few that remain (see Fig. 23). It is panelled and

Fig. 23.

moulded in the style we might expect at the Restoration period, and has a graceful open arcade to prevent the occupants from being entirely shut off.

There is a chair of the same period within the communion rails, and a chest under the tower : some of the nave pews deserve examination.

The font is plain and circular : it is smaller than mediæval fonts, and probably dates from the rebuilding period. It is interesting to observe that there has been an arrangement for locking the font,—an unusually late survival of the mediæval custom.

The exterior appearance of the church and its western tower is extremely plain and rude, and there is a great absence of the smaller features of a Gothic building—plinth mouldings, string-courses etc.—which so often give grace and dignity to a small parish church. Still the unusual features I have referred to lend an interest to the church, which is often lacking in more ambitious buildings.

The parish register dates from 1558.

Tugford.

St. Catherine.

THIS church, though small, is full of interest and is almost untouched by modern restoration. A chapel here is referred to as early as 1138. The nave of the present church was probably built before this, and the chancel some 50 years afterwards. The walls are continuous and the junction between chancel and nave is not well marked inside, though just discernible in the masonry; but outside it is very clear, a string-course going round the walls of the chancel alone.

Only one Norman window remains: it is in the north wall near the east end of the nave. The lancet east of this is the only original window of the chancel. Both are deeply splayed.

The east window is of three lights, and has the reticulated tracery so common in the middle and latter part of the Decorated period. The inner arch has curious shoulders, and a roll and fillet moulding round it. There are fragments of 14th century glass in the window. The windows on either side are earlier: each has a trefoil in the head above two uncusped sub-arches. Two early Decorated windows in the nave are similar to these, but the sub-arches are trefoiled. There are two single Decorated lights in the south wall, which have the sunk chamfer moulding outside. The one west of the door is cut into by a gallery, which is lighted by a plain late dormer window. This gallery is panelled in front with Gothic designs, partly Decorated and partly Perpendicular. It may perhaps be thought that these are portions of an old screen, but I am inclined to think they are post-Reformation and made for their present position (see pp. 11, 12). In this gallery are some remains of an old band-stand—a relic of the days when the organ was not the only instrument used in church services. The parish bier is an old one, and bears the date 1617. The font is a many hollow-sided bowl on a cylindrical stem: one part is divided from the other by a kind of broad cable moulding. The base is of Transitional character and the whole font is evidently of the same date as the chancel. This period is also represented in the beautiful south doorway. It is supported by filleted shafts : the abaci are square, but the moulding, though similar in form, is deeper than pure Norman would be. The western capital has undercut foliage and the one opposite is ornamented with a late form of scollop ending with rosettes. The hood-moulding is gone, but the heads which formed the ends remain. The porch is a nondescript erection of uncertain date.

The buttress against the south wall of the nave is of Early English form, and is of course an addition to the original building. East of this is a small recess with a wooden lintel : its object is not apparent. The larger recess east of this has been a doorway, which is curious, because there was originally another doorway just beyond. The latter has a tympanum ornamented with the cable, and foliage of almost Early English character. The jambs are chamfered, and everything fits in to the Transitional date already assigned to the chancel. The hood-moulding over this doorway has disappeared : it was a continuation of the string-course which goes round the chancel ; this is almost of Norman form and like the abacus shown in Fig. 10. In the south-east corner of the wall is an original recess. The arch has a roll and fillet and is supported by short columns, which have rudimentary foliage on the capitals and water hollows on the bases. It is certainly rare to find such external recesses at this period, though later ones are not uncommon, as at Shiffnal and Staunton Lacey. They were presumably for tombs.

The diagonal buttresses at the east end are of course not original. They were doubtless added when the east window was inserted. In a short length of wall the outward thrust of an arch over a three-light window cannot be despised : the earlier lancet form would not necessitate buttresses at the corners. The present window is Decorated in moulding as well as tracery—the sunk chamfer and wave moulding of 14th century character being used : the hood is of the scroll form. The cross on the east wall is apparently an ancient one.

At the east end of the north wall there is a recess which corresponds to that in a similar position in the south wall. West of this two recesses have been inserted in the 14th century, the moulding and feathering being Decorated. One of these contains a smaller recess with a gabled head, the use of which I cannot explain. The blocked north door may be original, but the plain semi-circular arch has no detail to prove that it is Norman.

The tower is at the west end and was added in the Early English period. The lower windows are broad lancets, and the buttresses of less projection than breadth. There are two buttresses at each west corner, the southern one being considerably enlarged for some unknown reason.   The tower arch inside is of no well defined type, but has nothing inconsistent with Early English date.   The western doorway has been somewhat restored.   High up on the west wall, the date 1720 is carved. At this time apparently the upper part of the tower was rebuilt.   The window is quite of 18th century character with a large keystone in the arch : the battlement is amusing.

The Perpendicular style does not appear to be represented at Tugford, but there is Norman, Transition, Early English, and Decorated of at least two dates.   The church is almost entirely covered with plaster inside and out, and this may have been intended originally.   One would like to see the roof opened out and a few other things done to the church, but one is grateful to the custodians for having preserved the building from the false "restoration" which has ruined so many interesting parish churches.

The registers are continuous from 1754, but the earlier ones are missing.

Wistanstow.

Holy Trinity.

THIS is a small but interesting cruciform building, dating chiefly from the latter part of the 12th century. There is no mention of a church in Domesday book, but a priest lived at Woolston in the parish, and was probably attached to this church. However, there are no 11th century remains, and most of the building was probably erected between 1180 and 1200. Some windows were added in the 13th and 14th centuries, and in the latter an addition was made to the central tower, and the arches below rebuilt: the nave roof belongs to the same period. As will be seen presently, certain repairs were executed in 1630, 1712 and 1800-2. In 1873-4 the chancel was restored under the direction of the late Mr. Pountney Smith, and the nave and transepts were repaired and the porch built in 1877-8. The lych gate was erected in 1887, and the vestry and organ chamber on the north side of the chancel in 1895.

THE CHANCEL.

The east wall has its original early lancets. The central one is higher than the other two : all are well splayed and very effective. There is another original window in the north wall, of Transitional character : the window itself is lancet-shaped but the scoinson arch is round. The other windows are insertions. The eastern one in the south wall is composed of three uncusped lights and is very similar to the east window of the south transept at Staunton Lacey, shewn in Plate XXV. In this latter case, the window probably dates from the 14th century (see p. 156), but such a form is of course Early English as a rule. The other south window is composed of three lights, with the mullions crossing one another in the head. The arches are acute and the form is one which was common when the Early English style was giving way to the Decorated. The same form on a larger scale may be seen at the east end of the south aisle of Worfield (see Plate XII.). The two-light window in the north wall is a nondescript form which may date from almost any period.

The roof was erected in 1630, when the old pitch was lowered, as is shewn by the fact of the beams not being clear of the window splays. There are four trusses : the two western ones originally had tie-beams, but these have been removed and collar-beams substituted of a similar form to the original ones on the eastern trusses. The date 1630 was carved on one of the tie-beams which was taken away. It has been re-cut on one of the collars, and in another place the date 1874 indicates the period of repair. Part of the ornament at the end of the beams is modern and part original.

THE NORTH TRANSEPT

contains two windows which are square-headed outside, and round and deeply splayed within. These windows might date from the early part of the 12th century, but they are a possible Transitional form, and there is no reason for supposing that the transept is earlier than the chancel. External evidence will presently shew that the north wall of the transept was rebuilt at the same time as the north window, which is a good early Decorated form. It has three lights, and, in the head, spherical triangles enclosing sexfoils.

The roof of the north transept deserves careful attention. It is a very simple one of the trussed-rafter variety and of five cants, but the interest lies in the probability that it is original, and therefore some 700 years old. The type of roof became common in the latter part of the 12th century, and, bearing this in mind and the fact that the mediæval roofs of the nave and south transept (which are not original) are of an entirely different kind, I see no reason for supposing that the north transept has ever had more than one roof. The pitch of the roof is at an angle of about sixty degrees : it is, as usual, put together with wooden pegs, without the aid of nails. The south end of this roof has been cut into by the modern staircase to the tower. Up to 1800 there appears to have been no external entrance for such a staircase, but at that time stone steps were placed against the west wall of the north transept leading to a door high up, which gave access to a children's gallery and to the belfry staircase inside. When the church was restored, the gallery and staircases were removed, the door blocked up, and a new entrance and staircase made in the south-west corner of the transept. The belfry doorway apparently dates from the early part of the century. The question naturally arises, how was the tower ascended originally? It cannot have been from the north transept, as the old roof, before it was cut into, would have prevented. There is no trace of a belfry doorway in the east, south, or west sides, and it seems almost certain that the approach was direct from below.

THE CENTRAL TOWER.

This brings us to consider the tower arches, and the signs they shew of masonry disturbance. Seven out of eight of the capitals, supporting these arches, have in their centre an inserted stone which does not fit well with the rest, and the eighth has an irregular appearance in the upper part. What do these scars indicate? If they had occurred on the east, north, and south sides only one might have supposed that screens had been placed in these positions to divide the chancel and transepts from the rest of the building. But they occur on the west side also, and one can scarcely suppose that there was a screen at the end of the nave in such a small parish church as this. A possible explanation is that there were beams resting on the capitals to support a rood loft, and that when these were taken away the holes were filled up by stones roughly imitated from the rest of the capital. There are of course instances of rood lofts under central towers, though one would not have expected so large a gallery in such a small church as this. The loft may have been approached from the north transept, for on the north side of the north-east tower pier some of the stones are rough, and look as if they had been corbels, now cut away, to support steps. There are two further scars in the masonry on either side of the chancel arch, which probably were made by the fixings of a screen. Another hole on the south side of the north tower arch may have been connected with a staircase to the belfry, which was reached directly from below, as already explained.

There is another point about these tower arches which needs explanation. The four arms of the cross date from the latter part of the 12th century, and yet these arches do not appear to belong to that period. There is no moulding on the arches which reveals the period, but what little is shewn on the capitals and bases points to a 14th century date. The moulding of the capital is rough, but the quarter-round under the abacus is Decorated so far as it goes, and the ogee curve on the simple base makes it quite clear that it does not date from the 12th century. We shall see presently that the upper stage of the tower was added in the 14th century, and, bearing this in mind, there is no great improbability in the idea that the tower arches were rebuilt at the same time,—an event which has often happened elsewhere.

THE SOUTH TRANSEPT

is doubtless of the same period as the north, though there is no characteristic detail to shew it. The narrow window on the east side has a depressed arch at the top, which may or may not be original, but the one opposite has a trefoil head of 14th or late 13th century date. The south window is Decorated, but later than the corresponding window of the north transept.

Instead of the geometrical form, the tracery here is reticulated: it has been renewed on the old lines. The roof is doubtless mediæval. It has tie-beams and collar-beams, and curved braces between the purlins. From the likeness of some features to the corresponding ones in the nave I should suppose it to belong to the 14th century, though it is not so fine an example.

The walls are almost covered with paintings, which were executed early in the 17th century. They were hidden till recently by whitewash, which was removed and the paintings restored in 1877-8. They comprise the Ten Commandments, the Lord's Prayer, the Creed, some texts, ornamental borders, and two shields, one of which has the initials "F P". The paintings in the nave and north transept were so far gone that they could not be renewed. They consisted chiefly of texts, but there was also a representation of the Royal arms.

THE NAVE

like the chancel and transepts is aisleless. It is only about six inches longer than the chancel, but the transepts are, as usual, considerably shorter. The broad lancet in the west wall has a modern head, but the jambs are old. The circular cusped window above is new: it replaced one of debased character. In the north wall is a narrow light with depressed arch, and opposite are two trefoil-headed windows of 14th or late 13th century date.

The remains of two other windows must be noted. One is a deeply splayed lancet over the blocked north doorway. It corresponds in form with the east windows, and is doubtless of the same date. It will of course be noticed that it is cut into by the doorway, which must therefore be later. The remarkable point, however, is that at the restoration, a similar window was discovered which was cut into by the south doorway. It was found difficult to display this window, but its existence shews that the south doorway is not original. Neither of the existing entrances to the nave therefore are of the same date as the walls, and it is almost certain from this fact, and from the irregular external appearance of the west wall, that the original entrance was at the west. The south doorway is clearly pre-Reformation, as there are remains of a stoup attached to its inner eastern jamb. The door with its simple ironwork may be mediæval, or of the same date as the lock, which has the inscription

    I P   C W   1696

The churchwardens of this year had the same initials, their names being John Poston and John Pinches.

The roof is one of the finest features of the church. It has tie and collar beam trusses alternately. Some of the beams are well moulded, and there are bold, if somewhat irregular, purlin braces in the form of quatrefoils. The upright panelling on the top of the walls has well-carved tracery of Decorated character.

The font is a somewhat small round basin on an octagonal stem, which rests on two steps. It is very plain. What little moulding there is corresponds with that on the tower piers, and both doubtless belong to one period.

THE EXTERIOR.

The modern porch replaces a very rude wooden erection which dated from 1733, as an entry in the churchwardens' accounts shews. On the gable of the south transept is the base of an ancient cross. Underneath is a sun dial, and below this the window with the reticulated tracery. It has the hood-moulding of the common Decorated form shewn in Fig. 14, E.

The central tower is not ornate, but the massive appearance is effective. The Transitional tower stopped above the lancet windows in the belfry storey. A change of masonry is noticeable, but there is little in the plain two-light windows above to reveal the date : this is probably shewn to be 14th century by the quatrefoil of Decorated character carved on the north-west pinnacle. The other ornamentation of these pinnacles may not be mediæval, for they were certainly repaired in post-Gothic times. The roof of the tower dates from 1712, as an inscription inside reveals.

The general appearance of Wistanstow reminds one of Church Stretton, which is partly of about the same period. Church Stretton is on the whole finer than Wistanstow, but the latter possesses a richer doorway. It is in the south wall of the chancel and is an excellent example of Transitional work. The hood-moulding is ornamented with the Early English dog-tooth : one of the terminations is a female crowned head. The doorway is once recessed and has plain semi-circular arches. These are supported by nook-shafts, the capitals of which are well carved with shell-like foliage, with a grotesque head on the western capital. The abaci are of the characteristic Norman form shewn in Fig. 10.

Buttresses were added to the east wall in 1873-4, when it was partially rebuilt.

The north wall of the north transept was evidently rebuilt in the early Decorated period. The corner buttresses are of two stages and have greater breadth than projection. This is rather an Early English characteristic, but the buttresses and the window between them may well fit in to a late 13th century date. The western buttress has been cut into by the steps already mentioned.

There is a good deal of interest in this small cruciform church, and a few of the architectural features are of real beauty.

The parish register dates from 1687.

CPSIA information can be obtained
at www.ICGtesting.com
Printed in the USA
LVOW13*1534300718

585375LV00051B/888/P